Mozart Symphonies

Stanley Sadie

STANLEY SADIE

MOZART
Symphonies

BBC MUSIC GUIDES

ARIEL MUSIC
BBC PUBLICATIONS

Published by BBC Publications
A division of BBC Enterprises Ltd
35 Marylebone High Street, London WIM 4AA

ISBN 0 563 12769 4

First published 1986

© Stanley Sadie 1986

Typeset in 10/11 pt Garamond by Phoenix Photosetting, Chatham
Printed in England by Mackays of Chatham Ltd

Contents

to Sir Denis Forman,
fellow-Mozartian

Introduction

In no substantial form was Mozart as prolific as he was in the symphony. He composed his first as a boy in London, probably in the summer of 1764, when he was eight; he composed his last, the 'Jupiter', in Vienna twenty-four years later. Although only a handful of his symphonies date from his full maturity, the collection as a whole represents him at many different stages of his development, especially his early development. During his childhood and youth, when – understandably – he was particularly susceptible to influence, he wrote symphonies not only in his native Austria but also in England, the Low Countries, Italy (Milan, Bologna and Rome) and France, and the music he produced reflects his flirtations with the taste of those countries.

How many symphonies did Mozart write? The question is not easy to answer; or rather, it can be answered in several different ways. Several early ones, probably, are lost – of two 'rediscovered' in recent years one is authentic, one almost certainly not – and a number of works that have some entitlement to be reckoned as symphonies are adaptations of music originally written for other purposes. And in a few cases there are doubts about authenticity. The old 'complete edition' numbered them up to 41 in the first place, including however two (Nos. 2 and 3, K.17 and 18) that we now know to be spurious, and another (No.37, K.444/425a)[1] of which only the slow introduction is Mozart's. The supplements to that edition include six further symphonies from the years 1767–72, numbered 42–7, and indeed numbers up to 55 have been assigned to other works, some of them of dubious authenticity, that might be regarded as Mozart symphonies. Among these are some ready-made symphonies that he drew for concert use from existing serenades, taking three or four movements from a work originally of seven or more (for example K.204/213b, 250/248b and 320); others are derived from overtures written for theatre works, usually with a new finale added for concert use. One could thus say that Mozart wrote something like sixty symphonies; but any such figure is somewhat arbitrary. We can however say that, of works composed as symphonies in the first place, there are forty-eight surviving (though there are doubts about the authenticity of four of them) as well as a few that are lost.

1 A number following the familiar 'K' is that assigned to the work concerned in the chronological catalogue of Mozart's works originally drawn up by Ludwig von Köchel and first published in 1862; where a second number is given after an oblique stroke, that is the number assigned to the work in the most recent (1964) revision of the Köchel catalogue.

The symphony as a musical genre has its origins in the Italian opera overture of the seventeenth century, and especially in the three-movement overture form, fast-slow-fast, that came to be preferred as that century drew towards its close. The three-movement symphony soon came to be used in a variety of contexts, ecclesiastical and courtly; and when the social changes of the mid-century led to the rise of the concert, private, semi-public or public, in which an orchestra almost always took part, the symphony became – as indeed it remains – the standard form for the principal orchestral item or items. By this time the four-movement symphony, including a minuet, was generally favoured, especially in central Europe. Often, in a concert, symphonies would be performed to open a programme and to close it, making up the solid fare that served as a framework for the various intermediate items (solos, vocal and instrumental, concertos and chamber works); sometimes a symphony was broken up and other works played between its movements. Mozart's symphonies written outside Salzburg, and those written in Salzburg for use outside, were intended as concert music. Those written in Salzburg for performance there were intended for use in concerts at the court of the Prince-Archbishop or for some other part of court ceremonial – including use during services, in the cathedral or elsewhere.

MOZART'S FORMS

Mozart's musical forms are referred to a good deal in this book, so a note about them and about how we discuss them may be opportune.

The basis of almost all musical forms in Mozart's time is what is generally known as the 'sonata principle'. This principle governs the design of individual movements, not of a work as a whole. In such movements, when the initial thematic material has been stated, the music moves from its home, or tonic, key to a complementary key (always, at this period, the dominant, the key a fifth higher, or in a minor key the relative major), where secondary material is presented. Later in the movement most or all of this material is likely to be heard again, now in the home key, thus resolving the structural tensions created by the original statement of some of it in a foreign key.

The first movements (and some other movements) of Mozart's mature symphonies, like those of other composers of his time, follow what is traditionally called 'sonata form'. A sonata-form movement falls into three main sections: the *exposition*, divisible into first subject (or theme, or group of themes), which constitutes the material heard in the home key, and second subject, which embraces the material stated in the dominant key (or relative major); the *development*, which may simply be an interlude but may restate, 'develop' or 'argue' material heard in the exposition; and the *recapitulation*, where the exposition material is reheard, all in the tonic. The term 'subject' – used because of the sense in which music may be understood to use its ideas as a basis for discussion – may stand for a single theme, or even a motif, but may also represent a whole section. (Some analysts, like Donald Tovey, have preferred to use the word 'group'.)

In his early works, and frequently up to 1774, when he was writing on a fairly modest scale, many of Mozart's first movements take a rather simpler pattern, akin to sonata form but recapitulating only the second-subject material. Such a form (sometimes called 'extended binary' or 'semi-sonata') successfully resolves the structural tensions and, as the generally brief development section commonly begins with first-subject material, possesses a certain symmetry. It lacks, however, the home-key recurrence of the opening music, which, in the larger-scale movements of the later Mozart or Haydn (and especially Beethoven), may provide a strongly-defined, climactic event. Occasionally, as we shall see, Mozart (and others) reversed the recapitulation, bringing back first-subject material close to the end of a movement.

All Mozart's symphony first movements follow these procedures. Most other movements use them in some degree; they were basic to a composer's way of thinking at the time. They appear in most of his symphony slow movements (a few follow a simple ternary pattern, *A–B–A*) and his finales, though in some of these rondo form (in which the main theme recurs in the home key, with intermediate episodes) is used. Minuets fall into a ternary pattern (minuet–trio–minuet); often each section has sonata-form elements on a miniature scale. Mozart never used variation form in his symphonies.

MOZART'S ORCHESTRA

The standard orchestra at any but the largest court in the eighteenth century consisted of strings, two oboes and two horns, with keyboard continuo. This was the group Mozart had available at the Prince-Archbishop's court at Salzburg, and the one that he could count on finding virtually anywhere he travelled; it is accordingly the group for which a large majority of his symphonies were composed. Often oboists could also play the flute, and composers sometimes asked them to take up the alternative instrument to provide a change of colour in a slow movement; more rarely he would ask them to use their flutes throughout, or to reverse the commoner procedure and use flutes in the outer movements and oboes in the slow movement. (As we shall see, matters of this kind would often depend on the key of a symphony and thus the notes that could be played on the natural horns, with which the woodwind instruments would mostly be coupled.) If a bassoon were to hand it would normally double the bass line; Mozart rarely supplied specific bassoon parts before 1773. Exceptionally, other instruments might be available: an extra pair of horns, flutes in addition to oboes, a pair of trumpets and timpani – these last were generally reserved for more brilliant or ceremonial works, for which players could be drawn in from a military establishment or a theatre orchestra. Normally trumpets and drums were used only in music in D, C or (more rarely) E♭. By the time of Mozart's later symphonies, from the end of the 1770s and the 1780s, a fuller selection of wind players was generally available to him.

The number of string players varied widely, from single desks or even one to a part up to fifty or more; the Salzburg court orchestra of the 1770s is documented as having about twenty-three (eighteen violins, two each of violas and cellos and one double-bass), while the Vienna court orchestra in the 1780s and early 1790s had about twenty (including two or three each of cellists and double-bassists). Orchestras were directed primarily by the leader and secondarily by the keyboard player, who normally supplied harmonic and rhythmic support, certainly in the tuttis and probably elsewhere too, on the harpsichord.

I am grateful to Alec Hyatt King for reading over the manuscript of this book and making a number of valuable suggestions. The book has also profited from the research, especially on matters of chronology, of Wolfgang Plath and Alan Tyson, and from the work of Neal Zaslaw, not only for his active role in the establishment of true texts for the symphonies and helping to put them authentically on record but also for many enthusiastic and enlightening conversations about them. I am deeply grateful, too, to my wife for her forbearance over my profligate consumption of the midnight oil while the book was being written.

Early essays, 1764–6

> In London, when our father was dangerously ill, we were forbidden to touch a piano. So, to keep himself occupied, Mozart composed his first symphony, for all the instruments of the orchestra – but in particular for the trumpets and kettledrums. I sat at his side and copied it out. As he composed, and I copied, he said: 'Remind me to give the horn something worthwhile to do!'

Thus Mozart's sister, Anna Maria ('Nannerl'), recollected in 1800 the creation of her brother's first symphony. If her memory was correct, the time was the summer or early autumn of 1764; their father Leopold was suffering from what he described as 'a kind of native complaint in England, which they call a *cold*', from early July into September. The eight-year-old boy (the advertisements say seven) had played concertos and solos, and improvised, at his previous London appearances; but on 21 February and 13 May 1765 the 'overtures' – or symphonies, for in this context the words are interchangeable – given at the Mozart family's concerts were all claimed as the boy's. These must have been the earliest public performances of Mozart symphonies.

There is evidence, from remarks of Leopold's, and from documents from the Breitkopf publishing house in Leipzig, that Mozart wrote four symphonies or more in London. Only three have come down to us; with these, as with others of his earliest works, it is impossible to know how much he may have been helped by Leopold, though by this date his father's help is unlikely to have amounted to more than advice over models and procedures and the correction of 'grammatical' solecisms. The models were the symphonies of Johann Christian Bach and Carl Friedrich Abel that he heard and studied in London (indeed he copied out one Abel symphony, which was for many years assumed to be a work of his own, No. 3 in E♭, K.18; No. 2 in B♭, K.17, is a work of Leopold's).

Although it does not conform to Nannerl's description – there are no trumpets or drums (unless they were written separately and are now lost), nor does he give the horn 'something worthwhile' – the E♭ symphony, K.16, has always been regarded as Mozart's first. Much of it, certainly, is elementary in style and content. It starts with a little common-chord fanfare, immediately dropping to *piano* for the contrasting phrase typical of the Italian-influenced J. C. Bach; and although the cheerful second subject and its continuation have plenty of spirit, much of the music echoes the patterns that a gifted, enterprising boy might discover at the keyboard. Many of Mozart's early sonatas show a similar preoccupation with textural patterns that accommodate changing harmonies. This applies equally to the little Andante, in C minor; the Presto finale, however, in the 3/8 metre popular with the pre-classical symphonists, matches the manner and especially the vitality of J. C. Bach's finales and has some fresh, imaginative touches. This symphony is not in itself a remarkable work, in no way superior to several hundreds of others of the time. What is astonishing is that a work of a nine-year-old should even call forth such comparisons.

The A minor symphony ('K.16a') recently discovered in Denmark, long known only by the appearance of its opening bars in a Breitkopf list, turns out to be hopelessly unlike Mozart (at any period) in its style and cannot be regarded as his. One of the London symphonies corresponds with the very J. C. Bach-like major opening in a Breitkopf catalogue, but the work as a whole does not survive. The remaining symphonies are works in D, K.19, and (only recently rediscovered) in F, K.19a. We have no means of knowing the order of composition of these London pieces, or how many more there may have been. But certainly these two seem much more assured than K.16. The first movement of K.19 already has the brilliance and hint of swagger that typify Mozart's extrovert D major music of later years, with its sturdy, fanfare-like unison opening set against *piano* phrases, and its energetic tuttis (even if the first of them is trite in content). There is a gentler second subject, as in all the symphonies in this group – Charles Burney thought that J. C. Bach was the earliest composer to use contrast as a principle (that is, as a principle of form) and it is doubtless his example that Mozart had in mind. The sudden unison, accented A♯ when the exposition has just ended, in A, provides a startling moment, analogous to the famous C♯ in the finale of Beethoven's Eighth, half a century later. The appealing lyricism of the Andante is again much in J. C. Bach's vein, using his favourite kind of imitation between instruments (note the expressive and original little cadential figure); and the finale is a bustling 3/8 Presto. Clearly Mozart had learnt how to establish and maintain the momentum and sense of direction of a movement. The F major work has some of the same qualities – perhaps less inventive vigour, but the forms are even more neatly articulated. Again we find scraps of imitative writing (see Ex. 1) and a melodic line of real tenderness in the Andante; Mozart's variety of texture in these slow movements shows a remarkable grasp of orchestral resource (note, for example, the flickering figure in the viola which so charmingly animates the texture). Again, too, there is a lively 3/8 finale, spirited and witty if rather over-dependent on sequence.

Ex.1

K19a, i.9

The Mozarts had travelled to London across southern and western Germany and through Paris; their first stops en route back to Salzburg were in the Netherlands. Because Mozart and his sister were taken ill, they were compelled to spend several months in The Hague, and it is to this time that Mozart's next two symphonies belong. He was just coming up to his tenth birthday when, in December 1765, he wrote K.22 in Bb. His command of musical material continues to increase. Here the opening phrase, with its *forte–piano* contrasts, is at once adapted to lead into a climax through a 'Mannheim crescendo'; it returns to introduce the development, is worked in the bass and then the violins, and a final appearance, back in the home key, rounds off the movement in dramatic fashion. This seemingly unorthodox formal arrangement may serve as a reminder of the clear links between early sonata form and the ritornello schemes of the late Baroque. The dialogue in the second-subject material here underlines the importance of siting the first and second violins on opposite sides: the pleasing echo effect becomes tautologous repetition if they are seated together. The rest of the symphony does not quite keep up this level. In the wistful G minor Andante there are some rather clumsy, naive punctuation points, but there is also a phrase (Ex. 2) foreshadowing a more famous G minor work. The finale, another of the 3/8 romps, draws its main idea from a J. C. Bach piano concerto (Op. 1 no. 6) – and passed it on to the Act II finale of *Figaro*, twenty years later.

Ex.2

K22, ii.16

Mozart's second Dutch symphony was written in the early weeks of 1766. We know from a remark of Leopold's that he supplied music for a festive concert on the installation of Wilhelm V, Prince of Orange; probably the divertimento *Gallimathias musicum*, K.32, which includes workings of Dutch folk tunes, owes its origins to that occasion, but the symphony, K.45a, may well do so too. This work, often called the Lambach Symphony (it was first known from a score at the monastery at Lambach in Austria), was for a time suspected of being a composition of Leopold's, but the recent discovery of an annotated copy puts its history and authenticity beyond question. Its likely origins may perhaps explain its rather formal character – the first movement is busy music, propelled more by rhythmic figures than by themes. But the unassuming, exquisite slow movement – essentially a line for muted first violins supported by pizzicato basses, a moving harmonic accompaniment on the inner strings, and sustained horns – more than makes up for any melodic deficiency elsewhere. The finale, the last in this 3/8 group, has a happily light touch in both texture and content.

Vienna, 1767–8

The Mozart family arrived back in Salzburg from their 'grand tour' at the end of November 1766. The following September they were off again, this time to Vienna; probably the intention was to take advantage of the crowds gathering in the imperial capital at the time of a royal wedding, but unfortunately the affianced archduchess succumbed to smallpox during an epidemic and died, and the city quickly emptied. Leopold Mozart rushed his children northwards, to Brünn (now Brno) and Olmütz (now Olomouc), where both suffered mild smallpox attacks. One or two symphonies belong to this period, K.76/42a and K.43, both in F.

The doubt as to whether it is one symphony or two concerns K.76, its date and its authenticity. We have no autograph score or supporting circumstantial reference for this work; it is known, and attributed to Mozart, solely on the strength of a manuscript once in the Breitkopf archives in Leipzig and now destroyed or lost. It has a number of peculiarities of style compared with the symphonies of the period that we know definitely to be Mozart's, sufficient to cast doubt on it though not to decree absolutely its expulsion from the canon. Its first movement has a curious lack of energy, partly perhaps because of its rather heavy wind textures – two oboes, two bassoons and two horns are called for, and, uncharacteristically, they are allowed few moments of rest during the fast movements. The actual invention too lacks real spirit. That is even more the case in the Andante, which is made up of little phrases that fail to cohere; it also has some strange pizzicato effects. There is a good minuet, in the true, hearty Viennese vein; it could be taken for a piece by the young Haydn. Some authorities have wondered if the minuet was a later addition, converting a three-movement work from the Salzburg months or even earlier into a four-movement one to suit taste in the capital. The finale is another oddity, starting with a quotation from a Rameau gavotte, from an *opéra-ballet*, and retaining a balletic elegance quite unlike the high spirits of Mozart's finales of the time. If this is Mozart, it is a piece well off the main lines of his development.

No such doubts, however, surround the fine symphony K.43, the first of his symphonies that needs no kind of apology on account of his youth. We have again the fanfare-like start, the contrasting phrase, the crescendo leading to a cadence on the dominant; then the modulation is carried through in a nine-bar tutti, the violins 'scrubbing', the basses developing the fanfare figure from the opening. The texture lightens for the gentler second subject, on upper strings alone; after that a powerful tutti follows, at first with sustained textures, then more open as the violins lead emphatically towards a cadence, and finally in unison. The development picks up the tutti with fanfare figures in the bass, but it is a little perfunctory, and we are soon back with the second subject in the tonic – which however is given a new twist to its tail, melodic, harmonic and rhythmic, a typical Mozartian device. Also very characteristic of Mozart, at all periods, is the subtlety of rhythmic structure. Nothing here sounds other than normally symmetrical in the musical phraseology; one would expect the music to be full of four-bar and eight-bar phrases. In fact there are also three-bar, five-bar, seven-bar, nine-bar and even eleven-bar ones. Further, the harmonic rhythms are managed in such a way as to give the music a strong sense of direction.

The Andante represents a more richly worked example of the type we saw in K.45a. Here, as Ex. 3 shows, the melody for muted first violins is supported not only by pizzicatos in the basses and seconds and moving harmonic accompaniment from the violas (which are divided), but also by sustaining horns and a soft halo of sound from a pair of flutes; the effect is charmingly fragrant. The music itself comes from a duet that Mozart had written in his little Latin intermezzo *Apollo et Hyacinthus*, composed for Salzburg University the previous spring. The minuet is more ordinary, perhaps a shade heavy, as apt for the dance floor as the

Ex.3

K43, ii.1

concert room; its pert little trio ends with a pleasantly graceful touch. The finale, in gigue-like 6/8, is a neatly worked out example of the extended binary type, with some witty byplay between the violins and a nicely poised cadential passage – another example of Mozart's early command of harmonic movement and timing.

The autograph manuscript of this symphony indicates that it was written at Vienna in 1767; Leopold, however, also noted 'Olmutz' on the score, so possibly it was begun in Vienna and completed during the eight weeks of enforced inactivity at Olmütz in November and December. On the way back to Vienna the Mozarts gave a concert at Brünn, on 30 December 1767, at which it could have had its first performance.

Eighteen days later, he had another new symphony ready: K.45 in D is dated 16 January 1768. This is the first Mozart symphony we have calling for trumpets and drums; it must have been written with a fairly large-scale concert in mind, though in fact they gave no performances until late in March when 'a grand concert' was held for the Mozarts at the house of the Russian ambassador. The music of the first movement is less focussed than that of K.43. It is adeptly written, but the themes are inclined to be scrappy and cliché-like, perhaps influenced by the style of the Italian opera overtures current in Vienna. One tutti, however, closely echoes the opening of K.45a with its tremolando violins above dotted rhythms in the basses. The movement's 'development' section is slender, a brief interlude rather than true development; but it is succeeded, for the first time in a Mozart symphony, by a reference to the first-subject material in the tonic – not truly recapitulatory, but still significant. The Andante, for strings alone, is slight but graceful. After another sturdy Viennese minuet (a sonata-form in miniature, incidentally) with a trio for strings alone, there is a finale in a contredanse-like style, musically uncomplicated, though the basses' taking up of the opening is worth noting.

A few days after completing this symphony Mozart and his father had an audience with Emperor Joseph II. Joseph, perhaps unwisely, suggested that Mozart might write an Italian *opera buffa* for production in Vienna; Mozart quickly composed *La finta semplice*, but because of various intrigues it remained unperformed, much to Leopold's indignation. For an overture Mozart simply adapted his latest symphony. In the light, presumably, of the orchestral forces he expected to have available, he removed the parts for trumpets and drums (they merely colour the music and have nothing vital to play) and added new parts for flutes and bassoons; he also added a couple of bars to the first movement to strengthen its main cadences, deleted the minuet, and adjusted the end of the finale to lead directly into the opening chorus. He also considerably refined the phrasing and articulation and altered some rhythms (his changes provide food for thought on matters of performing style). Later, he re-adapted the overture as a concert symphony by supplying a new four-bar close to the finale.

Partly because of the anxieties surrounding *La finta semplice*, the Mozarts remained in Vienna up to the end of 1768. One further symphony, K.48 in D, certainly belongs to this period (it is dated 13 December 1768: though why he should have wanted to complete a symphony just as they were leaving Vienna is a shade puzzling). Another, K.45b in B♭, is also generally supposed to have been written in Vienna during 1768. The only surviving copy of the work bears a note describing Mozart as Salzburg Konzertmeister (a post he acquired only at the end of 1769) and as 'Cavaliere' (a title he received from the Pope in summer 1770). Yet the music itself might well belong to these Viennese months. First comes a triple-time movement with some lively and bustling violin writing, a development a good deal longer than usual in which both first- and second-subject material are used, and a reversed recapitulation – that is, one that begins (as in normal extended binary form) with the second subject in the home key, but brings back the opening at the end of the movement. This is a device that the Mannheim composers in particular, and occasionally the mature Mozart, used with some dramatic force. It makes a pleasing effect here, if not a very strong one since the opening theme is not particularly striking and the late reappearance is slightly perfunctory. Probably Mozart was thinking more in terms of a codetta recurrence – which matches the return after the end of the exposition – than of finally producing the theme like a trump card. Another point of interest about this movement is Mozart's use, as bass to the main second-subject theme, of a four-note figure later to become famous as the fugue subject of the finale of his last symphony; some scholars have tried to read significance into this, but it is perhaps better to recognise that these four notes simply happen to make a natural bass to this particular melody.

The symphony continues with an agreeable, wholly unpretentious Andante in E♭, a sonata-form miniature. There is a sturdy, Viennese-style minuet; it is worth noting how Mozart averts rhythmic four-squareness by interposing a two-bar phrase between the pair of four-bar phrases that essentially make up the main idea. The trio too has a subtle touch, also a two-bar extension of an eight-bar phrase, done by repeating the melodic line but introducing a chromatic harmony underneath, to attractive effect. The finale, a vigorous sonata-form Allegro, has some sterling tuttis and an unusually full development of the opening theme.

If there are Viennese features in K.45b, in K.48 they are more numerous and more strongly marked. The first movement, again in triple metre, is in full sonata form with a development, again, almost as long as the exposition, and truly developing the ideas already heard (from both subjects). This is probably Mozart's earliest symphony in which the recapitulation includes the first subject (that is, the first in 'sonata form'); oddly, however, a prominent section of the second is omitted, though that may be connected with the fact that this material has already had a good airing in the development. The movement begins strikingly: the violins start with four dotted minims, descending from top D to middle C, then going on down to their lowest note before climbing back again, with alternate *forte* and *piano* to reinforce the drama. The second subject allows no contrast or relaxation, soon running off into 'rushing violin' passages of a kind beloved by Austrian church composers. The constant pounding quavers in the bass – these are sometimes disparagingly known as *Trommel-Bass* ('drum bass') – add to the sense of urgency. The Andante, for strings only in a simple texture, is by comparison quite ordinary though pleasant enough. There is a pompous and formal minuet, and a spirited, strongly directed gigue-style finale in 12/8 metre. Everything about this symphony shows that Mozart had assimilated the Viennese manner: the form of the first movement, the full and sustained textures, the rhythmic drive, the layout of the slow movement, the idiom of the minuet. The result is arguably the finest of his symphonies to date. Mozart's year in the capital had been well spent: he was beginning to build up a compendium of techniques and styles on which he could later draw at will.

When the Mozarts left Vienna at the end of 1768, Leopold Mozart wrote a petition to the emperor complaining about the intrigues that had prevented the hoped-for staging of *La finta semplice*. In it he attempted to rebut the charges of inexperience that, understandably, had been levelled at his son. He included a list of the boy's compositions to date, mentioning thirteen symphonies.

We may be reasonably sure that eight of the symphonies we have so far discussed belong to Leopold's thirteen: K. 16, 19, 19a, 22, 45a, 43, 45 and 48. Possibly K. 45b should be added, but we cannot be certain of its date. Another that can be added is K. 19b, which is almost certainly authentic but is lost. K. 16a may be excluded. Some works to be discussed later in this book may be earlier than we have supposed. Leopold's count may include pieces originally composed as overtures for dramatic or other works: the titles symphony and overture were virtually interchangeable. The Köchel catalogue includes a further five symphonies that are known only by their opening bars; most look fairly plausible and some at least could be early works. Much must remain doubtful, at least pending further discoveries. But the eight of the thirteen that we can identify with some confidence provide us with a firm basis for understanding how far Mozart had gone with the symphony at the time of his thirteenth birthday.

Italy, 1770

The Mozart family were back in Salzburg early in January 1769. They remained at home for less than a year. Leopold had long intended to visit Italy, and was eager to do so while his son was still young enough for his talents to arouse wonderment; he must also have been keen to visit the land that was everywhere regarded as the main source of musical novelty. Many German composers of previous generations had done so, to their benefit: Handel, Hasse, Gluck and J. C. Bach, for example.

So the Mozarts, father and son, set off in the middle of December. They gave a concert in Verona, and another in Mantua, which began with two movements of a symphony by Mozart and ended – three concertos, two sonatas, various vocal pieces and sundry improvisations later – with the third movement. This must have been a symphony Mozart had brought with him from Salzburg; if it was a four-movement work, the minuet must have been left out to suit Italian tastes. The Mozarts travelled on to all the main Italian cities, including Milan, where the Austrian minister, member of a Salzburg family, proved a valuable friend, and where they met G. B. Sammartini, the senior figure among Italian symphonists. They spent four weeks, in April and May, in Rome; on 25 April Mozart wrote to his sister: 'when this letter is finished, I shall finish a symphony of mine, which I have begun . . . one symphony is with the copyist (that is, my father) – we don't want to send it out to be copied as it would be stolen.' They spent most of the summer near Bologna, from where, on 4 August, Mozart wrote to his sister: 'By now I have composed four Italian symphonies.'

What is an 'Italian symphony'? A symphony written in Italy? A symphony in three movements (as opposed to an Austrian one, usually in four)? Or simply a symphony in the style favoured in Italy? This last explanation seems to fit in the best with Mozart's way of thinking and his understanding that taste varied from place to place. And it fits too with the symphonies we believe him to have written there. Our information about which symphonies belong to these months is undependable, but the weight of evidence suggests that one of the Roman symphonies is K.81/73l, for which there exists a set of parts marked 'Rome, 25 April 1770'. On K.84/73q we have seemingly contradictory information, for the score is marked both 'Bologna, July 1770' and 'Milan, Carnival 1770'. The Mozarts had been in Milan at the end of the Carnival season, in January and February. K.84 could belong to that time and have been revised at Bologna in July; alternatively, it could have been composed during the summer and performed in Milan at the next year's Carnival, which began in December 1770. Or one of the inscriptions could be mistaken. These two, however, are almost certainly among the four that Mozart referred to in his Bologna letter; there are half a dozen from which the other two could be chosen, but the likeliest candidates are a pair of works, like K.81 and 84, in D major and closely akin to them in style. These are K.95/73n and 97/73m.

The key of D major is itself a significant choice. This is traditionally the most brilliant orchestral key. It is one of the easiest and most effective for the violins, allowing simple fingering patterns, plentiful use of open strings and easy, resonant multiple stops. It is also the best key for trumpets, should the composer want them. It is no accident that nearly all Mozart's orchestral serenades, intended for outdoor performance, are in D major, or that he wrote more symphonies in D than in any other key.

All four of these works are composed in a much simpler style than Mozart's earlier symphonies. Their themes are more like figures than melodies, falling into neat, symmetrical patterns (Ex. 4 shows two typical examples). We have seen, in some of the earlier works, how Mozart varied the metric structure by means of uneven phrase-lengths; this scarcely ever happens here. Almost every phrase in these four symphonies is four bars long, with few of the subtle elisions that create variety in most of Mozart's music, earlier as well as later. Harmonically, too, the music is uneventful; the kinds of melodic pattern used by Mozart encourage static harmony and regular tonic–dominant alternation. Even the orchestration is unadventurous: the line of the music is carried almost exclusively by the first violins, with simple accompanying textures in which the oboes and horns do little in the fast movements but sustain the harmony in tuttis. With themes that are essentially violinistic tags, the scope for development is small. In the first movements of K.81 and 84, the exposition is linked to the recapitulation by a brief, relaxed interlude on a dominant pedal (one is twelve bars long, one ten); K.97 offers something more dramatic, with sharp dynamic contrasts and chromaticisms. It is perhaps to be expected that in K.95, where the first movement is not in full sonata form, there is allusion to the first-subject material.

But it would be mistaken to regard these symphonies as notably inferior because they fail to show some of the traditional features of interest. They are remarkably brilliant and spirited pieces, deftly written to answer a particular need. Mozart's models are plain: one only has

Ex.4

K95, i.1

K81/73l, iii.49

to listen to symphonies or opera overtures by such men as Piccinni, Pai-
siello or Sarti to understand what he was aiming at. And in some
respects he surpassed his models. His command of effective instrumental cliché – an important part of any composer's equipment – is
remarkable; the music moves purposefully, and the form is crystal clear.
There are some charmingly witty touches and an occasional, welcome
moment of softening, notably in K.84. Of the slow movements, the
K.81 Andante offers echo effects between first and second violins
(stressing once more the importance of having them sit on opposite
sides) and draws the oboes into a dialogue with them, if not one of much

consequence. Those of K.84 and 97 have a certain gentle grace but are not helped by their rather predictable, four-square phraseology. In the Andante of K.95, which follows without a break on the first movement, the oboists take up their flutes to add colour and delicacy to the music's unassuming lyricism.

In a postscript to one of his father's letters home, at the end of the summer, Mozart wrote to his sister: 'We wish that we could introduce the German style of minuets here in Italy, where the minuets are so long that they last nearly the length of a whole symphony.' He may have been referring, as the context implies, simply to dance music; but it is possible that he had in mind the extended minuet-finales that some Italian composers favoured in their symphonies. In two of the symphonies of this group, K.95 and 97, he included minuets; it has been suggested that these were later additions, when he wanted to use the symphonies in Austria, but there is no evidence for that and their direct, vigorous style is of a piece with the remainder of the works concerned – though the D minor trio in K.95 provides a moment of contrast with the prevailing D major jollity. Jollity is of course the rule in the finales. In K.81 we are back in the 3/8 hunting mode; it was, after all, from Italian-influenced symphonies that Mozart originally picked up this style. Here he delightfully varies the ebullience with a witty and fleet-footed second subject (Ex. 4*b*). There is wit again in the running triplets of the finale of K.84 and in the *piano* echoing of a noisy tutti. The 3/8 type crops up again in K.97, a fairly substantial sonata-form movement whose second-subject theme seems to hint at Beethoven's Seventh Symphony. This work calls for trumpets as well as horns. K.95 is exceptional in lacking horns altogether; it acquires a bright, brittle orchestral palette from the use of trumpets in their stead in the fast movements.

As we have seen, there is no firm evidence for dating any other particular symphonies of Mozart's to his first Italian journey. But if we recognise the kinship of the four works just discussed, we may reasonably add to them K.74 in G, which has a good deal in common with them stylistically. Its first movement especially is in their manner, with themes that are little more than scraps of figuration succeeding one another in two-bar or four-bar phrases, often repeatred. Possibly there is a touch more of lyricism to the second subject here, but it is short-lived, overtaken by another crop of semi-thematic tags. Exposition and recapitulation are linked by a four-bar series of sequences on the oboes (the only time they are heard independently) and a two-bar lead-in. As in K.95, the first movement leads directly into the second – another piece

of evidence that the symphony is an Italian one, for this was the preferred form of the Italian opera overture; indeed someone (possibly
Mozart) wrote on the autograph 'Ouverture zur Opera Mitridate', then
crossed out the last three words. Mozart's *Mitridate* was given at Milan,
as the climax of this first Italian tour, at the end of 1770; it has its own
overture, but it is perfectly possible that this piece was initially
intended in that role.

The slow movement is an unassuming 3/8 piece in sonata form (with
no development); it is distinguished to some extent by its main second-
subject idea, which has a hint of the minor mode, warm textures and
alternating *forte* and *piano* bars. The best movement is certainly the
finale, marked 'Rondeau' and beginning, on the violins alone, in the
style of a contredanse. This witty, spirited piece sports enough of a
French accent to justify its heading, and traditionally to the French contredanse it is duly in regular rondo form. There is a curious second episode in G minor, faintly exotic with its snapped rhythms and its
pizzicato accompaniments; it would not be surprising if the violin
melody in the middle turned out to be a local popular tune.

Finally, there is the C major symphony, K.73. Its dating has long
been in question: the autograph is marked – not by Mozart – 1769, but
there are some odd clues to suggest a later date: Leopold copied a few
bars from the bass part on to a sheet where Mozart worked a musical
puzzle that he met only in 1770, and a jotting of a theme from the symphony appears on the manuscript of some minuets of early summer
1772. The latest handwriting research – Mozart's writing developed in
very clear-cut ways around this time – suggests 1770 or even 1769. The
music has a good deal in common with that of the Italian symphonies,
and the finale is a companion piece to that of K.74, another *contredanse en
rondeau*, more extended this time – its pattern is A–B–A–C–A–D–A,
with the final episode a gently amusing minor-key one. Otherwise, this
earliest survivor among Mozart's C major symphonies is a somewhat
showy, pompous piece; Mozart was inclined to use this key for music of
a martial character – it was good for trumpets and drums (they are
included here) and more solid, less dashing than D.

The first movement opens with a flourish around the common chord
of C, then at once sets against it a couple of bars of counterpoint, almost
Corellian in manner, for the strings. There are some noisy tuttis, in one
of which the violins play busy tremolandos above a rather static bass
theme. There is not much that one could call a tune. But the Andante,
where the oboists take up their flutes, is a charming, song-like piece, for

25

the most part a violin melody with flutes an octave above and a light accompaniment below. The horns and trumpets, as so often, rest during the slow movement, but they are back to add their tone of emphasis to the minuet and of course the finale. There are features here to suggest an Italian symphony, but the energy and the sturdiness do have an Austrian ring too. Just conceivably, it could have been composed in Salzburg for use at those first Italian concerts.

Salzburg and Milan, 1771

The Mozarts began their homeward journey from Milan, with *Mitridate* safely and successfully launched, in January 1771. They visited Turin and took a month in Venice on the way, arriving back in Salzburg only at the end of March. By then plans were already afoot for another journey to Italy: a theatrical serenata had been commissioned from Mozart for a royal wedding in Milan in October. So after little more than four months at home Mozart and his father set off again – it was always necessary for a composer of a major theatrical work to arrive early at the place of performance so that he could hear the singers and tailor the arias to their voices. During the weeks in Salzburg he certainly composed one symphony, possibly as many as three; while he was in Milan he wrote certainly one and possibly two symphonies as well as a movement to make up a third. Then, back in Salzburg by the middle of December, he completed another symphony before the year was out.

The first symphony to be discussed in this chapter is the one in B♭ numbered K.74g. This is one of the works that was long known only by a catalogue entry and then rediscovered in a manuscript copy. There is no firm authentication, in the form (for example) of an autograph or a copy annotated by Leopold, but nor is there any special reason to think it other than a genuine work of Mozart's. It is necessary to make this point as the editors of the sixth edition of Köchel assigned it, for reasons that they kept to themselves, to the appendix of doubtful works, which is why it is sometimes called K.Anh.11.03. We do better to keep to the Köchel third edition number, which reflects the editor Alfred Einstein's belief that the work dates from early summer 1771. Dating on the basis of style is notoriously risky – we now know that Einstein made many serious errors – for Mozart's stylistic development was neither smooth nor consistent. And though it is reasonably safe to take note (as in the last chapter) of the impact that meeting a new musical style might have upon him, as well as his recognition of the need, when in Italy, to do as the Italians did, by the next year he was already well on the way towards a synthesis in which the Italian symphonic tradition was just one element.

The Italian element is strong in K.74g. The work begins, however, like the Viennese K.48 – in triple metre, with one note to a bar; the recurrence of the opening idea as part of the second subject is also more Viennese (and in particular Haydn-like) than Italian. But the slender textures and the themes that are not much more than violinistic tags, as well as a blandly interludial development (an inconsequential eight-bar phrase, heard twice over, then a two-bar lead-in), all have much in common with the D major symphonies we looked at in the last chapter. However, the extra momentum that results from triple metre seems to give K.74g more weight than those works. This and the graceful Andante are both in full sonata form. There is a brief, sturdy, four-square minuet, with a gentle trio whose second half springs some delightful, chromatic surprises: this if nothing else should settle any residual doubts as to the work's authenticity, so accomplished and so typically Mozartian is the passage. The dashing Allegro molto finale is again in sonata form, with a brief 'false recapitulation' – not so characteristic of Mozart, it should be said – after four bars of development; development quickly resumes, though it is over-dependent on sequence. It is inviting, in view of the stylistic mixture, to associate this spirited symphony with the weeks when Mozart, back from Italy, was feeling himself an Austrian again; but the actualities are never quite that simple and it could well belong rather earlier.

But K.75 in F, another symphony that may putatively be assigned to the middle of 1771, could scarcely have been written earlier; nor does it show any Italianisms. The orchestral texture of the opening bars is something altogether new (see Ex. 5), with the line of the music shared between violins and oboe. And some of the second-subject material (Ex. 6) embodies something close to imitative writing. Although the tuttis here are in the usual style, the interest in a well-worked texture remains – the 20-bar development has the air of string quartet music, with its interweaving lines (based incidentally on fresh material). The whole symphony gives an impression of being carefully and thoughtfully composed. The minuet – exceptionally, it is placed second – and its trio are each economically built around a single phrase, repeated and slightly varied; and in the Andantino, a gentle sonata-form miniature in which muted violins draw a fine line of melody, the lower parts of the texture are more interesting, more positive in their contribution, than in earlier movements of the kind. The finale, also in small-scale sonata form, is a jolly, dance-like movement in 3/8, notable for the curious cadence to its main theme – delayed by a rhythmic hiccup by which the phrase is converted from eight bars to nine.

The one symphony we know for certain to come from these intermediate Salzburg months is K.110/75b, in G. Mozart himself dated it July 1771. It begins with another triple-metre movement, with the same kind of cheerful swagger that we met in K.75. This work's open-

Ex.5

K75, i.1   (+ 8ve lower)

Ex.6

K75, i.20

(+ 8ve lower)

ing tutti, marked *forte*, lasts thirty-six bars before we have a *piano* eight-bar respite for the principal second-subject theme; then the tutti resumes, including a restatement of part of the opening theme to lead to the close in the dominant. The 'development' itself is mostly an interlude (it ends with a brief tutti echoing one in the exposition); but when we reach the turning-point of the recapitulation – the point where the music is adjusted to remain in the tonic instead of moving to the dominant – Mozart interpolates something more like real thematic development, having the violins, which up to now have almost wholly been in unison or simple harmony, take a snatch from a linking theme and base a dialogue passage on it. The insertion of development at this point is a device very characteristic of Haydn; in fact the manner of the movement as a whole, with its strong momentum and its almost unrelieved tutti scoring, is markedly Viennese.

This movement is written for the usual wind instruments, oboes and horns, as are the minuet and the finale. But the slow movement unexpectedly calls not only for flutes (which as we have seen the oboists would play) but also a pair of bassoons; presumably they had been assumed to be doubling the string bass instruments in the fast movements where no specific parts are provided for them. They add to the attractions of this pretty movement with their occasional octave doublings of the violins and their enrichment of the middle texture, while the flutes add a surface bloom to it. The minuet sharply recalls Haydn (Symphony No. 44, for example) with its canonic imitation between melody and bass (Ex. 7); this vigorous music is contrasted with a gentle E minor trio section with string quartet-like textures. The finale is in the contredanse pattern again, and again in rondo form, less extended than the similar finale of K.73 but again with its final episode in the minor. There certainly seem to be some strong family resemblances between the three symphonies of this group, even if in reality they may not be a group at all.

Tradition has it that the symphony K.96/111b, in C, belongs to the time that Mozart and his father spent in Milan during the autumn of 1771 for the production there of Mozart's serenata *Ascanio in Alba*, though there is no particular evidence for that date. There is, in fact, no decisive evidence that this symphony is his at all; no autograph exists, nor any authenticated source, and the style and content certainly leave room for doubt. The symphony is in the rather heavily pompous mood that we have seen is associated (not only by Mozart) with C major. Its first movement begins with fanfarish phrases and a loud tutti, with a

Ex.7

K110/75b, iii.1 (+ violas 8ve higher db 8ve lower)

etc.

sudden change of pace to its surface activity when it ends and some unusual harmonic progressions in the tutti that follows. There is an abrupt close to the exposition, a brief development and a rather cursory recapitulation. Still less characteristic is the C minor Andante, which takes its line and its melodic expression from the Baroque siciliano tradition. Neither the minuet nor the finale has quite the technical polish of even the most ordinary of Mozart's works; listen for example to the awkward rhythm of the cadences in the trio.

Alongside this strange piece, K.112 in F, the symphony we know Mozart to have written in Milan (there is a dated autograph), is a small masterpiece. Its first movement has the rhythmic swing typical of Mozart's best triple-metre music, the tuttis are full of inventive ideas, and the second subject is a delightful dialogue between oboes (with violas) and violins, wittily carried off; the shape of the exposition is neatly articulated by the conjunction of emphatic or spirited material with gentler and more lyrical. In the Andante, a song-like movement for strings alone, textures are again used to mould the form: at first there is a melody above semiquaver 'Alberti' patterns, then a more sustained dialogue between first violins and seconds with violas, and finally (after a few bars of simple accompanying textures) Mozart arrives at a favourite eloquent texture, with the violins in octaves and the violas a third below the seconds. This creates a natural point of climax to end the exposition. There is a minuet and a 3/8 finale, less rumbustious and more shapely in detail than those of his childhood days.

When he was still in Italy, Mozart made up another symphony. Opera (or serenata) overtures of the day were often in two or three movements, so could be detached from the parent work, perhaps fitted out with an extra movement, and used as concert symphonies. Mozart, as we shall see, did this on a number of occasions. The first such occasion on which he had to supply a new movement was when, in Milan, he adapted the overture to *Ascanio in Alba*. This consisted originally of a lively, lightweight Italian Allegro, in very much the manner of the symphonies in D we looked at in the last chapter, and a miniature Andante grazioso to which, in the serenata, the Graces danced; this led into the first chorus. To turn the work into a usable symphony, all he had to do was add a finale. This he did (K. 120) – a bubbling little Presto in the same vein as the first movement and in a slightly truncated sonata form.

Salzburg, 1771–2

The Mozarts arrived back in Salzburg in the middle of December 1771. This time they were at home for ten months before the third and last of the Italian journeys, during which Wolfgang's opera *Lucio Silla* was given at Milan. No fewer than eight symphonies belong to this period.

The first of them, K. 114, was completed before the year was out. It is in A major, a key which carries particular implications about the use of the orchestra in Mozart's day. Natural horns could sound only a limited number of notes; to make the instruments as useful as possible the composer would require them to be fitted with crooks – lengths of tubing joined on to the main body of the instrument – that enabled them to sound those notes in the key of the piece. For music in A major, a short crook had to be used and the horns would play at a higher pitch than usual. This lent a special colour to the orchestral tuttis, and it also inclined composers to use flutes in place of the oboes to procure a better spread of registers in the wind section. Music in A, accordingly, often has a softer and warmer orchestral tone than music in other keys; it is no coincidence that A major is the key that Mozart (like many other composers) chose for almost every love-duet in his operas.

In K. 114, then, Mozart reversed the common procedure, using flutes in the quick movements and oboes in the slow one. The symphony begins, however, with the violins alone, *piano*, giving out an eight-bar melody of quite an original cast. This melody, repeated and rounded off by the orchestra, is taken up, almost in fact developed, in the tutti that ensues; it steers the music to E major for a new theme with repeated notes and expressive appoggiaturas, and a hint – memories of the J. C. Bach style that Mozart had used seven years before – of contrapuntal imitation, now much more expressively handled (Ex. 8). A phrase derived from this theme is worked into the texture of the tutti that now ends the exposition (Ex. 9). The 'development' is interludial, allowing the wind instruments, and the violas, their moments of prominence; there is an orthodox recapitulation.

The violas have another moment of prominence in the Andante, where they are divided to add extra richness to the texture. Again the movement is begun by violins alone. There is an expressive second subject, based (as in the first movement) on appoggiaturas, and an interesting development – the falling fourth of the movement's opening is counterpointed by a smooth theme in quavers, which when the fourth drops out takes the music over. The minuet is enlivened by some

Ex.8

K114, i.36   (+ 8ve lower)

Ex.9

i.47   (+ 8ve lower)

pseudo-emphatic chromaticisms and has a charmingly witty A minor trio where the interest lies less in the near-monotone melody of the first violins than in the running triplets of the seconds. This inventive symphony ends with an Allegro molto appropriately lighter in character but with hints of drama here and there.

The first symphony of 1772, Mozart's most prolific year as a symphonist, was written in February; this, K. 124 in G, is a jolly piece for one composed and perhaps performed during Lent. The first movement, in triple metre, has a splendid swing to its rhythm and a number of passages around the second subject that hint at the figurations beloved of *opera buffa* composers. By now, Mozart's development sections are generally rather longer; this one is thirty-six bars, of which, however, only the central dozen use material from the exposition. After an Andante, and a stop-and-start minuet, there is a rondo finale, whose ten-bar phrases, touches of dialogue, and curious coda (where for bars on end almost nothing happens) round off the symphony a shade surprisingly.

The C major symphony, K.128, the first of three he wrote in May 1772, is another with a triple-metre first movement, but it is less obviously energetic than most, held back by its triplet motion; it does however achieve a kind of energy in its second subject, with a striding theme on the violins (Ex. 10a), which is characteristically given a hint of ambiguity in its echo (Ex. 10b). If once again the development neglects to develop the ideas, that is slightly compensated for by Mozart's little diversion in the recapitulation, where he takes the first theme off into A minor and F major to provide a better key balance. The Andante grazioso that follows (in G rather than F – Mozart rarely prefers the dominant to the subdominant for a slow movement) is written in a careful, string-quartet style, with shreds of imitative writing and significant contributions from the middle voices; and although the finale (there is no minuet) is a noisy jig, it too has passages of refined part-writing, as well as a fanfare of horns to round it off. One sees in these works how Mozart, now sixteen, is beginning to draw together elements from different styles.

Ex.10

(a) Allegro maestoso

K128, i.27

(b)

i.38

The next work, K.129 in G, illustrates this further. It begins like a lightweight Italian piece; but then its second subject is made up (very charmingly) from a figure used in imitation, with a Mannheim crescendo to follow – and moreover the movement has a fullness of texture and strength of impulse which are wholly Viennese. The slow movement, in C, is gracefully devised from phrases that are really no more than clichés; and the finale is in the vigorous 3/8 vein we met earlier, now worked out at greater length (more than 200 bars, though admittedly short ones) and with greater sophistication – but also, interestingly, reverting to extended binary form rather than full sonata or rondo.

The third of the symphonies dated May 1772, K.130 in F, has a number of specially interesting features. Its mood at the start is akin to *opera buffa*: the figure made up of staccato quavers with a little jerk (a Scotch snap) at the beginning of each bar could serve to accompany some kind of bustling or mischievous stage activity. The second-subject material is similar: first a theme with trills (repeated with echoes on the second violins), and then an idea based on the opening one. The work, unusually, calls for a pair of flutes instead of oboes, and an extra pair of horns – these, an afterthought (they are separately written into the score of the first two movements), are keyed in high C, strenuously high for the players who had to use a crook still shorter than for the parts for horns in A in K.114. There are four horns in the Andantino too, a movement notable for its odd phrase structure. The opening theme, for muted violins, has two three-bar phrases, then a four-bar one, and with these short, 3/8 bars the effect is slightly abrupt. It is even more curious that, when a version of this theme appears at the beginning of the development, Mozart has 'normalised' it to four-bar phrases. Another oddity is the coda to this movement, where the horns and the flutes are allowed prominence to present some quite ordinary ideas; this is followed by a brief reminder of the opening theme, first *piano* on the violins, then (on the second time only, if the repeat has been observed) on the whole orchestra, *forte*. The effect is so strange that one wonders if some private allusion is built into the music.

The minuet, like others we have looked at, gains vitality from a bass-line that imitates the melody. The trio is another oddity, with its strangely shapeless melody (in pairs of three-bar phrases) and its few bars of perilously high horn writing. After this, one might expect an eccentric finale, and there is no disappointment. Its chief eccentricity (besides the three-bar phrases in the second subject and the codetta) lies in its length and indeed its symphonic weight. Though a spirited and sometimes witty piece with its echoes and its disarmingly direct themes, it is an extended movement, running to nearly 200 bars and giving an impression of taut, purposeful organisation. This symphony seems to herald for Mozart the move (affecting other composers of the time too) towards more substantial finales, movements to counterbalance the greater intellectual weight traditional to the first movement rather than simply supply light relief after it, and as such representing a significantly different way of thinking about music as entertainment – or something more than that.

The next symphony, one of two composed in July 1772, is another work with unusual features and simply as music rather more interesting than K.130. K.132, Mozart's first Eb symphony since K.16, begins with a favourite Eb cliché of his, familiar from the K.482 Piano Concerto and with a family resemblance to the two-piano concerto (more distantly to other works). This too calls for four hornists: if Salzburg had a pair of visiting virtuosos in May, they stayed on, and had to stretch their lips still further for this piece which calls for horns of a kind unknown, in high Eb. In fact this is a little pointless, for Mozart never asks them (as Haydn did his hornists) to gambol among the leger lines.

The first movement is a broad, well-proportioned Allegro, whose 'development' makes no attempt at developing or even touching on anything already heard but fills in thirty bars with innocuous material, happily throwing the listener's notice on to the logic and timeliness of the recapitulation. Mozart wrote two slow movements for this symphony. His first version (scholars have differed over which came first, but there seems no doubt – the New Mozart Edition notwithstanding – that this is correct) is a 3/8 Andante, beginning with a melody derived from Gregorian chant: the standard plainchant, in fact, for 'Credo in unum Deum'. This must surely be taken to imply that the symphony was at some time used, or intended to be used, in church. It makes a slightly strange classical slow-movement theme, but Mozart works it into the context well enough, supplying a confidently normal answering phrase – and in the recapitulation he even, adventurously, extends the plainchant quotation. Mozart was not the only Austrian composer of his time to quote chant melodies; Haydn did so in several works, of which Symphony No. 26 (the 'Lamentation') is the best known. Mozart's alternative slow movement here, a 2/4 Andantino grazioso, could perhaps have been intended for use where an ecclesiastical reference would have been inapt. It is arguably a superior piece, in any case, having a violin melody of exquisite gentleness and a happily textured accompaniment, with moving middle strings (the viola occasionally pre-imitating the melody) and the oboes and horns adding their voices, mostly in alternation.

The minuet begins with the violins chasing each other, and the basses join in too; once again there is an odd trio, a strange non-melody in the first violins with a plain harmonic accompaniment. One is bound to suspect, both here and at the equivalent point in K. 130, some private significance, whether it be to some concealed melody, ecclesiastical or with some local or personal meaning, or just a musical joke. Certainly there is jocularity in the finale, another movement in the gavotte-like rhythm of the *contredanse en rondeau*. This one acquires an extra bucolic touch from its scoring: the main theme is played each time with the violas doubling the first violins an octave below, with solid chords on the oboes and horns to stress the rhythm and supply harmonic reinforcement. Of the three episodes in the rondo the central one, in C minor and with some curious 'snapped' rhythms, is particularly adventurous.

For the other symphony of July 1772, K. 133, Mozart turned to D major and the brilliant style associated with that key. But this symphony is altogether more spacious and more richly worked than earlier examples. It is also formally unorthodox. The music at the opening – it sounds like a Mannheim crescendo, but takes a different turn – is not heard again until the very end of the movement: this is an example of the 'reversed recapitulation', a device favoured at Mannheim, which we met briefly in connection with K. 22 (p. 13). Whether such movements are in a modification of sonata form or an augmented version of extended binary (or even in some relic, as could be argued, of Baroque ritornello form) is a nice point; the fact that the option can be discussed underlines the futility of taking form classifications too seriously. A movement like the first of K. 133 lacks the dramatic double return of the tonic key and the opening material, but it has its own, more rhetorical kind of drama in the 'triumphant' reappearance of the opening music to round the movement off. The music itself impresses for its vigour above all, especially in the tuttis with their rival wind fanfares (trumpets versus the oboe-horn ensemble), their sturdy violin lines and their striding basses; momentary relief is supplied by the main second-subject theme, with its perky Scotch snaps (or Lombardic rhythms, as they are sometimes called) and by the *opera buffa*-like theme, with its sharp little trills, of the closing section. From all this, a three-note upbeat figure, heard in various contexts, emerges as the main talking-point of the development.

The Andante is a pretty, graceful piece for a single flute (generally playing an octave above the first violins) and strings, in unusually open textures – the basses are mostly *pizzicato*, the violas largely tick away in accompanying semiquavers, and the seconds are much of the time in dialogue with the firsts and the flute. The gentleness is emphasised by the muting of the violins. The trio of the minuet, after those of the last two symphonies, seems normal – if the first violin line looks initially unprepossessing that is because it is serving as part of a contrapuntal fabric: simple, graceful, partly contrapuntal writing at a modest dynamic level was one of Mozart's favourite ways of counterbalancing the noisiness, the drive and the homophonic textures of the traditional minuet. Finally there is an energetic 12/8 jig, of the same family as the K.48 finale but, drawing on Mozart's much increased arsenal of effects, it uses contrapuntal means at a number of points to add to the music's impetus.

We end this group as we began it, with a symphony in A major of great originality. Like K.114, K.134 (written in August 1772) calls for flutes and horns, but here in the Andante as well as the rest of the symphony. It does not, however, begin *piano* but rather with a strong, direct statement of its principal theme (Ex. 11). The tutti that follows after a *piano* restatement has the opening figure (*x* in Ex. 11) in the basses and the second violins. There is a lighter second-subject theme, part of which is given out *forte* in a tutti; then *x* returns, first to underpin a tutti, then in two statements of the first four bars of Ex. 11 (a *forte* unison, echoed *piano* by the violins alone), and next in the last bars of the exposition. Virtually the entire development, too, is based on *x* and Ex. 11. After that, a 'double return' would be not only devoid of drama but also redundant; so Mozart goes straight into the second subject – and then interrupts it with the tutti built on *x* that we heard close to the

Ex.11   **Allegro**

K134, i.1

beginning of the movement. After a diversion to A minor for more of the second subject, the movement resumes a normal course – though at the end, rather curiously, there is a coda, recalling none of the earlier themes, but with a hint of D major that helps to balance the movement's tonalities. This detailed description may give some idea of how closely allied are thematic material and structure, and how structure can be moulded – within certain limits – to accommodate new types of idea and the treatment arising from them.

The Andante touches on new depths of feeling for a symphony slow movement. Its melody begins with a phrase that must have held a special significance for Mozart; he used it several times, for example in his bassoon concerto and in the Countess's first aria, 'Porgi Amor', from *Figaro*. This last context may offer some clue as to the nature of its special significance. Here it is presented in soft, warm texture, with the second violins accompanying in 'Alberti'-type figuration and the flutes and violas adding gentle comments between phrases. The second subject moves more quickly and leads to a little climax of activity. The development is open to criticism for its diversity: it contains four distinct ideas, none of them related to themes already heard, within twenty bars. But if the result is that greater stress is laid on the main thematic ideas, no one need complain. The minuet follows what has become a fairly regular pattern, boisterous in the main part, unassertive and with a light dash of counterpoint in the trio. The violins alone lead off the finale, a movement positively bubbling with high spirits in its witty rhythmic figures, its syncopations and its mock counterpoint; but even when Mozart is teasing, the music is artfully and skilfully made, and here the re-use of the opening theme in the second subject and the closing section (analogous to the procedures in the first movement) holds the music firmly together. When, in October 1772, Mozart set out for Italy for the third and last time, he had acquired mastery over a new range of techniques and a maturity that finds a clear reflection in the enlarged scope of the music he was now ready and able to compose.

Salzburg, 1773–4

Mozart and his father arrived home from their final journey to Italy in the middle of March 1773. By the end of the month he had another symphony completed; two more, it seems, followed in April and a fourth in May. In outward features at least, all these have Italian echoes – each has three movements, and there is no shortage of brisk, mechanical figuration. Indeed one of them, K.162 in C, which is thought to date from April (for some reason the date written on the score has been almost totally obliterated), consists of very little more than figuration. Although neatly, even wittily put together, its first movement is really a collection of clichés; its most curious feature is the beginning of the recapitulation with bar 13 of the exposition, omitting the opening idea – which is however briefly alluded to at the very end of the movement (this is a simplified version of a formal device we met earlier: see p. 18). The Andantino grazioso, though enriched by divided violas and generous oboe writing, is hardly less slender in thematic appeal; there is a lively jig finale, deftly, even gracefully, carried off.

The C major work uses trumpets as well as horns, so has something of a festive character. The G major work, K.199/161b, probably from the same month, is a gentler-toned piece, without trumpets and with flutes instead of oboes (as the high key invites). The triple-time first movement has a firm sense of direction, maintained through the suave second subject and the emphatic tutti that follows it (any hint of pomposity in that tutti is quickly dispelled in its hushed echo), and even through the interludial development – which by this date is beginning to seem a little old-fashioned. In the slow movement, again an Andantino grazioso, all seems quite easygoing, with just a hint of sentimentality in the chromatics, until the second-subject theme comes to an end with a strikingly interrupted cadence, glancing at distant keys and darker chromatic implications – though Mozart, of course, brings us back without allowing too severe a disturbance to the elegance of the entertainment. The finale begins with a skittish piece of two-part counterpoint, the main theme of which is borrowed, consciously or otherwise, from the beginning of the symphony (see Ex. 12a and b); what is more, Mozart pursues the same theme for his lyrical, contrasting second subject (Ex. 12c), a charming piece of economy, humour and ingenuity. The counterpoint is not, however, merely a joke, as he makes abundantly clear in the recapitulation, where he extends it into a real, vigorous piece of 'working out', drawing the movement together much

41

Ex.12

(a) Allegro

K199/162a, i.1

(b) Presto

violins

K199/162a, iii.1

(c) Presto

strings *p*

iii.25

in the way Haydn was to do in some of the symphonies and quartets of his maturity. This is no embryo 'Jupiter', but it does show Mozart using contrapuntal writing in a new way, and certainly pointing in that direction.

The D major symphony that followed in May, K.181/162b, pursues the style of the C major work: in other words, here is another of those works full of brilliant writing and 'effective' passages, built up into an elegantly and logically shaped edifice of some size (a third as long again as K.162) but of modest substance. This is especially true of the first movement, with its violin tremolandos, its dashing semiquaver passages, its insistent figuration, its rhetorical dynamic contrasts, its pert little *piano* second subject. It is formally akin to K.162, too, though here it is only the first four bars of the exposition that fail to appear, and the material omitted is so inconsequential that it is more like a haircut than a decapitation. Yet the 'double return' is still noticeably absent. At the end of the movement, Mozart continues with the material of the development opening, as heard earlier, to form a link with the (once more) Andantino grazioso. This is another oddity: its first subject is a fairly ordinary twelve-bar theme for the strings, its second a somewhat extended elaboration of it for solo oboe, in *siciliano* style, with string accompaniment; after a five-bar link there is a recapitulation, in which the first subject is unchanged but the second recast so that it remains in the oboe's most expressive register. This leads directly into the finale, a lightweight sonata-rondo (A–B–A–C–A–B–A) in quick march rhythm. For all the thinness of this symphony's thematic matter, the piece leaves a reasonably satisfying impression because of the strength and vigour of its structure.

Why, one may wonder, did Mozart write symphonies at this stage in which the three movements are continuous, in the manner of an Italian opera overture? We do not know; but what we do know is that the symphony he wrote in March – easily the strongest of this group – was in fact used in a theatrical context, whether designed for it or not. In 1779–80 the Mozarts became friendly with Johann Böhm, manager of a travelling theatre troupe, and Mozart apparently consented to Böhm's using this work, along with some pieces he had composed for a play, *Thamos, König in Ägypten*, as incidental music to *Lanassa*, a drama by K. M. Plümicke after a French tragic drama set in India. If one imagines Mozart looking through his portfolio of symphonies with Böhm in search of something suitable, it is easy to see why this one, K.184/161a in E♭, should have been their choice. It has a fiery beginning (Ex. 13), repeated chords in a martial rhythm – typical, as we saw with K.132, of Mozart's E♭ openings – followed by a broken-chord figure for the violins, then striking chromatics, *forte–piano* alternations, sturdy unison tuttis and a powerful momentum. It is formally ingenious, too: the exposition ends (and the development begins) with Ex. 13 in the dominant, followed by a short modulating passage closely based on the music that earlier succeeded Ex. 13, and quickly leading back to a full recapitulation. And when that ends, the music goes as before, with a further appearance of Ex. 13, now of course back in the tonic. But this time there is a different continuation, leading us to C minor for the Andante, a deeply-felt piece whose principal idea is a five-note rhythmic figure, worked in various ways, mainly in imitation between first and second violins but also (in the tuttis) between the firsts and the wind ensemble. The climaxes at the ends of the exposition and the recapitulation have considerable passion,

Ex.13

K184/166a, i.1

amply warranted by what has passed. There is a lively 3/8 finale, but by no means a throwback to the earlier type; it is a well worked-out piece, with a spacious, quite lyrical second subject (note the touch of colour added by the doubling flute: this work calls for flutes and bassoons as well as oboes) and a highly energetic development, full of contrapuntal interest in its first half and enlivened by large leaps for the violins in its second. It must remain a puzzle why so fine and original a piece should have been closely followed by three that often are of only routine quality.

For the sake of completeness, another symphony needs to be mentioned at this point: K.141a in D. This is one of those works that Mozart put together by adding a finale (K.163) to two existing movements (K.161). He had written a serenata *Il sogno di Scipione*, K.126, for some Salzburg event in mid-1771 – not, as has until recently been supposed, for Colloredo's installation as archbishop in 1772; during 1773 (or possibly 1774) he took the two-movement overture, a lightweight D major Allegro and a slower movement in minuet-like style, and joined to them a spirited, scurrying Presto in 3/8 in a brilliant and occasionally witty Italianate manner.

In the summer of 1773 Leopold Mozart took his son to Vienna; we do not know the purpose, but may infer from cryptic remarks in Leopold's letters home that there were hopes of some kind of court appointment for Mozart. Any such hopes were disappointed; but the ten weeks in the imperial capital do not represent time wasted. Mozart wrote a set of six string quartets there, K.168–173, which clearly show him reacting to Haydn's latest quartets (Op.20) and to other Viennese music. So do the symphonies of late 1773 and 1774.

There are five of these, of which two were written within days of Mozart's return to Salzburg. One is K.182/173dA in B♭, which has a cheerful, bustling first movement with a second subject full of 'Scotch snaps' and a rather inconsequential development; the Andantino grazioso that follows, however, is a delicate, Dresden china-like miniature in which flutes and muted violins play together and in dialogue (its form can equally be construed as sonata or rondo), and the work ends with what is the last of Mozart's 3/8 finales. This piece was completed on 3 October 1773; two days later Mozart had finished his next symphony, a work of quite different temper and the earliest of his symphonies that can be reckoned an unquestioned masterpiece.

This is the G minor symphony, K.183/173dB, known as No. 25. It is his first in a minor key (indeed only his second full-scale minor-key work, the first being one of the Viennese string quartets – though the overture of his 1771 oratorio *La Betulia liberata* is in D minor). Minor keys were less used by composers of the early Classical era than by the previous, Baroque generation (men like Bach and Vivaldi); to the Classical composer the choice of key had greater inherent significance as regards the mood of a work, and a minor-key one is likely to be serious rather than frivolous, passionate rather than playful or brilliant. Commentators have naturally wondered what can have impelled the eighteen-year-old Mozart to write such a work at this particular moment. Was there some kind of 'romantic crisis' in his life, some kind of new awareness, to turn him in this direction? If so, we know nothing of it. Better, perhaps, to seek for parallels in the music he was encountering. Of them there is no shortage; minor-key symphonies, rare in the 1750s and early 60s, began to appear more often in the years around

1770. Haydn's Nos. 26, 39, 44, 45, 49 and perhaps 52 come from the five years before Mozart's G minor K.183; so do G minor symphonies by Vanhal and J. C. Bach. He may well have known some of these and, characteristically, have felt challenged to try his hand at the same kind of music. This wave of minor-key symphonies, most of them in G or D minor, has been seen as related to the *Sturm und Drang* ('Storm and Stress') movement in German literature of the time – exemplified in the early works of Goethe – and in the visual arts.

The influence of the *Zeitgeist* and the desire to emulate may, then, help explain why Mozart chose to write this kind of symphony. But it would be wrong to suppose that he was a stranger to music of an impassioned nature in minor keys; there are scenes calling on this vein in his operas *Lucio Silla*, composed a year before, and even *Mitridate* (1770). This G minor symphony, however, unmistakably breaks new ground. The opening four-note phrase (Ex. 14), with its bold, almost Baroque line heightened by the agitated syncopation of the upper strings, proclaims a different world from the formal, courtly openings we have considered up to now; and the continuation with leaping arpeggio figures and unison phrases, enhanced by the clanging chords of four horns, drives the novelty firmly home. And when the music cools, at the end of the first subject, it instantly heats up again with the second, with its emphatic phrases treated in imitation against tense tremolandos. This passage, which inaugurates a stormy tutti, turns out in the event to be only the first part of the second subject (a method Mozart was to use again); there is a rather lighter, more *opera buffa*-like theme to come, though even this, on its *forte* repeat, seems to acquire more weight and tension. The development begins, as often in such a movement, with a passage in contrapuntal imitation, here between violins and basses; but the music calms quite soon, if only so that the arrival of the recapitulation has due force. The key structure usual in a minor-key sonata-form movement means that – unless the composer turns finally to the major (as Mozart never did) – the second-subject music originally stated in the major is heard ultimately in the minor: and this, especially in a context like the present movement, is apt to provide a strongly pessimistic slant, with the only hint of light, as it were, finally extinguished. Certainly the *opera buffa*-like theme seems far less *buffa* on its final, G minor appearance. No doubt to ensure that the movement carried its full weight Mozart, exceptionally, indicated that both halves were to be repeated. And at the end he supplied an extra coda, quoting the opening theme – a procedure that he used in several of the symphonies of 1773.

Ex.14

Up to this date, Mozart had specified the inclusion of bassoons in the orchestra in only a handful of his symphonies. In the slow movement here, for the first time, he assigns them an important, melodic role: they echo the main theme, or counter it in some other way, phrase by phrase. The eighteenth-century bassoon was a soft-toned instrument (one English writer, around the middle of the century, said it was the only wind instrument that could happily blend with the strings), and the effect of these three-note phrases, with their dissonant appoggiaturas, on muted violins and then (marked *fp*) on bassoons an octave lower, is gently sombre in expression. The second subject is given to a fuller tutti, but it lasts a mere four bars. In the development the three-note theme is the topic of a sixteen-bar discussion; but the recapitulation is tellingly given extra expressive weight by the incorporation of an extra, eight-bar passage which takes the opening of the development as its starting-point and modulates freely through several keys – the insertion of a modulating passage of this kind was one of Mozart's favourite ways of giving the final part of a movement a stronger tonal focus, which it does by enhancing the sense of reaching the home key.

For the minuet we are back in G minor, with austere unisons answered by pleading, chromatic phrases: the idea of the minuet as an idealised dance is far away. The trio moves to G major and to the wind instruments – the preferred Salzburg wind divertimento combination, for which Mozart was to write half a dozen pieces over the next few years, of pairs of oboes, bassoons and horns, playing music of a balmy sweetness that briefly softens the mood rather than truly contradicts it. The finale is firmly back in the tense and serious world of the first movement, with its urgent, *piano* unison opening, repeated in the basses in the ensuing tutti with agitated syncopations above. Again the moment of relaxation afforded by the major key and the lyricism of the second subject are quickly forgotten when another, similar tutti follows (this time with the second violins assigned a sharp, snapped figure that recalls the first movement's second subject). This time, however, the development is hardly contrapuntal, but it is long and emphatic, with its material only remotely derived from what we have already heard. Again, the recapitulation's unbending adherence to G minor imparts an additional severity; and Mozart's intention that the movement have ample substance is once more made manifest by his indication – even more unusual in a finale – that both halves be repeated.

What is probably his next symphony – as we shall see, there is a shade of doubt as to the date of K.200/189k – is another remarkable work. K.201/186a, best known as No. 29 in A and dating from April 1774, is no less personal in tone than the G minor work, indeed in a sense is more so because it goes beyond the expression of strong passion in the customary language of the time. No. 29 (from now on we shall use the familiar, though of course incorrect, serial numbers in preference to the less familiar, and chronologically still incorrect, Köchel numbers) is hardly less passionate than the G minor, but at the same time it is more intimate, more chamber-music-like, more refined in its expression. It achieves its intensity in subtler ways. The opening bars are typical (Ex. 15). Here we have a simple idea, scarcely a 'theme', consisting of a dipping octave and an appoggiatura figure, in a straightforward series of rising sequences; but its repeat, in octaves and in imitation with the lower strings, imparts to it a new drama and intensity. There is a central lyrical theme to the second subject group, among various other ideas – the proliferation is typical, and does not the slightest damage to structural cogency; very characteristic is the beginning of the last tutti of the exposition, with the ascending chromatic notes on tremolando violins, again adding to the intensity. The development, however, is relatively relaxed and makes virtually no reference to material previously heard. This might seem like an opportunity missed; yet we have already had plenty of development of the main theme (and more is to come), while the secondary themes are scarcely susceptible to it. The recapitulation is orthodox; then, as in the G minor work, we have a coda incorporating a further appearance, with a little fresh development, of the opening theme. Once again Mozart draws on the effect of a late return of a movement's initial idea, using his experience of the drama of the 'reversed recapitulation' type to get the best of both worlds and pull the movement's threads firmly together.

The Andante, with muted violins, is an intimate, unassuming piece, for the most part a flowing melody on the first violins (sometimes the

Ex.15

K201, i.1 (+ 8ve lower)

b.13 (+ 8ve lower)
(+ wind, sustaining 8ve A's)

seconds take over, and the firsts add a gloss; sometimes the line is shared in dialogue). The type is familiar but the depth of feeling is new. And the melody is abundant: a first subject in dotted (even double-dotted) rhythms, and two distinct second-subject themes, one of them echoed with oboe. None of these is used in the development, which takes off from the triplet figure of the codetta, keeping it going in the second violins. It is worth noting how Mozart extends the first-subject material in the recapitulation, giving it a twist to G major and heightening the intensity with sharp, *forte* exclamations between *piano* phrases. Again both halves are repeated, and there is a coda where first the oboes and then the violins – their mutes quickly removed, to add brilliance after the subdued colours of this Andante so far – finally present the movement's opening couple of bars to round it off decisively.

The minuet begins quietly, but is full of martial dotted rhythms, echoed on the wind instruments to conclude each half; these aptly contrast with the soft-toned, lyrical trio. The finale is hugely spirited music, drawing on the manner of the old 'hunting' finales but now with real symphonic force: this comes partly through the nature of the ideas themselves, partly through the astute management of harmonic pace which guides the music so strongly towards its cadence points, and partly through the sturdy and tonally well-directed development section (based wholly on the opening idea). Yet again both halves are repeated and the first theme reappears in the coda: this scheme is becoming almost a cliché in the symphonies of 1773–4. The upward-rushing, unaccompanied violin scales at each formal junction point are a remarkable and arresting feature of this movement.

The remaining two symphonies of 1774 are altogether more relaxed. No. 30 in D, K.202/186b, composed only a month after No. 29, was surely intended as a festive piece; its cheerful extrovert manner is that of the Austrian serenade tradition, and it is at least as close in style to the Finalmusik serenade, K.203/189b, that Mozart wrote during the summer for the university end-of-year celebrations as to any other symphony. It calls for the same orchestral forces, pairs of oboes, horns and trumpets, as the Finalmusik, and the tuttis in particular – one with imitation between violins and basses, one with the violins declaiming a high melody while almost everyone else is in dialogue below, on a trill figure – speak of festive ebullience. Yet its ideas are well worked out, and the main second-subject theme has a certain symphonic seriousness along with wit and elegance. The development is closely argued, on a new phrase – which Mozart brings back in the movement's final bars (no recall of the opening this time, nor would so dramatic a gesture be appropriate in this lighter context). There is a graceful Andantino for strings alone, pleasing and unpretentious, and a sturdy minuet close, again, to the serenade manner. The finale moves even closer, with its dotted rhythms, its contrasts of the lively and the hushed, the slightly facile sequences of its second subject and the noisy tutti to end with. And its development embodies one of Mozart's most charming sallies of wit in its dialogues on a simple dotted-rhythm figure, varied in dynamic level and in the use of oboe and horn. Here we are back to the 1773–4 pattern of both repeats and a coda quoting the opening bars (after which it fades gently away) – these opening bars, incidentally, resemble in rhythm and thematic outline those of the first movement, but it would be ill-advised to regard this as more than a mild coincidence since no others among Mozart's symphonies show anything of the sort and the ideas in question are late eighteenth-century common coin.

The autograph score of Symphony No. 28 in C, K.200/189k, was dated by Mozart or his father, but someone since has done his best to obliterate the date: the month is clearly November, but the day, though probably 12, could possibly be 17 and the year might be 1773 or 1774. The later date is generally thought the likelier. This symphony, calling for the same orchestra, with trumpets, as No. 30, is broadly similar to that work in its style, although it tends to be more intimate, more akin to chamber music, at times. The trilling violin figure that responds to the opening statement of a C major triad immediately suggests a degree of refinement, as too does the principal second-subject theme, for the violins shared with the oboes. But here the development is based on material from the exposition, mainly the trilling theme (which readily lends itself). This is another movement where Mozart asks for both repeats to be made, as he does too in the slow movement and the finale. Here his device of bringing back the opening theme has a double signifi- cance, as he does so before the repeat mark rather than after: first time, it leads naturally on to the development, which (as we have seen) uses the same idea, and second time it provides the now standard, effective rounding-off. The Andante, with muted violins, is a gently appealing song-like piece of no special subtlety, while the most interesting feature of the minuet is the little echo on the horns that twice links the hearty opening four-bar phrase with the softer succeeding one. The Presto finale again features violin trills in helter-skelter music that scarcely pauses for breath – not even in the development which, based on the trill figure, is wittily elided into the recapitulation; Mozart lets the recapitu- lation creep in unannounced, forgoing the opportunity for drama in favour of a surprised realisation on the listener's part that the moment has come and gone. The coda, yet again, incorporates a final, emphatic reappearance of the music that began the movement.

These works brought to an end a prolonged and intensive spell of symphony composition: something like thirty new works over five years (a striking rate that, if continued over a working lifetime, would have made Haydn's output seem almost puny). Mozart did however require some symphonies, it appears, during the next year or so; besides using orchestral movements from serenades, he twice more converted opera overtures. From 1775 come a comic opera for Munich, *La finta giard- iniera*, and a pastoral drama written for the Salzburg archbishop's palace, *Il rè pastore*. The former has a two-movement overture, a brilliant and bouncy Italianate Allegro in D major followed by an Andantino grazioso, to which he subjoined a sparkling little 3/8 Allegro,

K. 121/207a, with more ingenuity in its development than he had previously provided in pieces of the kind. For *Il rè pastore* the situation was
slightly different, for here the overture was in only one movement. The
opening aria, however, is an Andantino for high voice, whose music
readily transfers to the oboe – which, with flutes and horns in the
orchestra, stands out suitably. The aria had originally led into a recita-
tive, so Mozart had also to supply a new ending to link it with the new
finale. This time the finale is an extended sonata-rondo, nearly 350 bars
long, but light and tuneful and in the rhythm of a contredanse – we saw
earlier, in the 1772 symphonies, how rondo form and contredanse style
were associated. The result is attractive if musically a little slender. But
that adjective is not one we are likely to require again.

Paris and Salzburg, 1778–80

Since 1772, Mozart had been a salaried *Konzertmeister* at the Salzburg court. The title is not specific: a *Konzertmeister* might be the leading violinist in the orchestra, or he could be a keyboard player with directorial responsibilities. From 1779 until his resignation in 1781 Mozart occupied the latter role, but during the period we are at the moment concerned with he was chiefly if not exclusively employed as violinist. It is surprising, then, that he had no cause to write symphonies in the mid-1770s, when his main works for Salzburg were in the sphere of church music and lighter instrumental pieces like serenades and divertimentos.

It took his 1778 visit to Paris to provoke another symphony. The previous autumn he had set out from dreary, provincial Salzburg (as he saw it) to find a post worthier of his gifts. He went to visit relatives at Augsburg, then to the Munich court, and on to Mannheim, but at both these last two he was politely turned down. At Mannheim he dawdled, for reasons musical and amorous; it took a stream of furious letters from Leopold to push him on to the French capital. There he duly made contact with the best-known, if not the best, concert-giving organisation, the Concert Spirituel, and was invited to write a symphony for performance at their Corpus Christi concert on 18 June. On 12 June, he wrote to his father that the symphony was just finished and he was 'quite pleased' with it. But he professed to care little whether it also pleased the audiences ('I can answer for its pleasing the *few* intelligent French people who may be there – as for the stupid ones, I shall not reckon it too great a misfortune if they don't like it'). He went on, however, to make it clear that he had tried to meet the Parisian taste: 'I haven't left out the *premier coup d'archet*! – and that's enough. The oxen here make such a fuss of this! – the devil! – they all begin together – just like in other places.' The Paris orchestra, famous for their power and precision, liked a tutti passage in unison at the opening of a work so that they could show off their technique and ensemble playing. In his next letter, written on 3 July, he gave a fuller report:

At the rehearsal I was very worried, as never in my life had I heard a worse performance; you can't imagine how, twice over, they scraped and scrambled through it. – I was truly most upset – I was eager to rehearse it again, but there were so many other pieces to rehearse, and no time left; so it was with a heavy heart and in a restless, angry mood that I went to bed. The next morning I decided not to go to the concert at all; but in the evening the weather was fine, and I decided to go, and that if it was going badly, as at the rehearsal, I would go up on to the platform, and take the violin out of the hands of M. Lahoussaye, *first violin*, and direct it myself. . . . Right in the middle of the first Allegro, there was a passage that I knew must please, all the hearers were quite carried away – and there was a great burst of applause – but I had known, when I wrote it, what kind of effect it would make, so I brought it back again at the close – when there were shouts of Da capo. The Andante also pleased, but above all the last Allegro – as I had heard that all the last Allegros here, like the first, begin with all the instruments together, usually in unison, I began mine with the two violins alone, *piano* for the first eight bars – after which came a *forte* – this made the audience, as I expected, say 'Ssh' at the *piano* – and then came the *forte* – when they heard the *forte* they at once began to clap their hands – I went as soon as the symphony was over to the Palais Royal – I had a large ice – and I said the Rosary as I had vowed.

It is clear from this letter that in reality Mozart cared very much what kind of impression the symphony made; and the music itself, quite different in scale and in manner from anything he had composed before, bears this out. Since his previous symphony he had not only three and a half years' additional maturity; he had also visited Mannheim, a leading centre of orchestral music, where new styles were being developed – styles particularly favoured in Paris, where the Mannheim composers often appeared (and where their music was chiefly published). He had been there many years before, but the renewal of contact with the excellent musicians at the court and the chance to hear the fine orchestra helped prepare him towards composing a symphony in the manner the Parisians demanded.

The Paris Symphony, No. 31, K.297/300a, is – predictably – in D major, the key above all for brilliant and effective orchestral writing. It was written for a larger orchestra than Mozart had ever used before, with a pair of clarinets as well as flutes, oboes, bassoons, horns, trumpets and drums besides the strings, which numbered something like twenty-two violins, five violas, eight cellos and five double-basses (probably the bassoons and possibly some of the brass instruments were doubled). Mozart particularly relished the sound of the clarinets in the orchestral tutti; on his way home from Paris he referred, in a letter to his father, to the 'noble effect' of a symphony with flutes, oboes and clarinets. His writing for the clarinets, understandably, is cautious, and he rarely uses them outside the tuttis; but there they supply a new richness and glow to the textures.

In a letter he wrote just after the première of the symphony Leopold remarked that, to judge by the symphonies from Paris he had seen, the Parisians 'must be fond of noisy music'. Mozart's Paris Symphony is quite noisy. It has fine, stirring tuttis, with a vigorous line for the violins and the kind of active bass line that lends great animation to the music (unlike the harmonically static, repeated-note bass-lines that Mozart, like other composers of the time, often used in his earlier symphonies). The actual thematic material in the movement, however, is relatively conventional, more a matter of figures than of melodies; but there is no development as such and most of the working-out of the ideas takes place at their presentation.

The one idea that runs through the movement is that of the *premier coup d'archet*. This is no more than four repeated D major chords, followed by an upward scale. As if to cock a snook at the idea, Mozart immediately follows it with a *piano* phrase for the violins alone. But he does in fact turn the notion of the dramatic *coup d'archet* to musical advantage, characteristically: he uses this particular phrase several times in the course of the movement, always at a critical juncture – to herald the second subject, as the main prop of the tutti closing the exposition, to begin the development and to carry through its main modulation, to bring in the recapitulation (inevitably), to mark the tutti in which the recapitulation diverges from the exposition, and finally to close the movement. It becomes, in fact, a device for drawing the movement firmly together.

Which, one may wonder, was the idea that Mozart 'knew must please', and reintroduced near the end? Probably it is one of the second-subject themes: the section starts with a brief dialogue passage where the woodwind answer a string phrase, then moves on to a seven-note figure, repeated to changing harmonies, and assigned to the violins in octaves with the violas another octave below. This unusual and effective three-octave texture resumes after a brief tutti with a new idea, presented with a different twist each time (see Ex. 16), and culminating in teasing music that raises the tension and demands release with the ensuing tutti. The fact that Mozart presents this phrase only once in the exposition but twice in the recapitulation (the reverse of what might be expected) suggests the more strongly that he set special store by it; further, the tension is engendered first time by a melodic sequence and

Ex.16

K 297, i. b.84

b.238 p

b.257 p

its attendant harmonies but second and third times by a tonic–
dominant progression repeated eight times over with a long crescendo
and a build-up of orchestral forces. There are some other differences
between exposition and recapitulation, of which one small example is
worth noting. The very first tutti in the movement includes an emphatic little phrase in dotted rhythm: in the recapitulation Mozart deleted
it from its former place, saving it instead for the very last tutti. This not
only shows a perhaps unexpected degree of deliberation in Mozart's
planning but also in a modest way foreshadows his technique, important in the great piano concertos of the 1780s, of rearranging musical
ideas in different orders for reasons of form and expressive effect.

'The Andante also pleased', Mozart had reported on 3 July. Six days
later (these letters, incidentally, bear the tragic news of Mozart's
mother's last illness and death in Paris), he told his father that it had not
much pleased the Concert Spirituel impresario, Joseph Legros:

He said it had too much modulation – and was too long – but all this was because the audience forgot to make as much or as long a noise with their applause as they did for the first and last movements – but the Andante has given the greatest pleasure *to me*, to all connoisseurs, music-lovers and most of the audience – it is just the opposite of what Legros says – it is entirely natural – and short. – But to satisfy him (and, he says, several others), I have written another one – each is appropriate in its own way – for each has its own character – but the later one pleases me the more.

The familiar slow movement, the one almost always played with the symphony, is a 6/8 Andante (marked Andantino in the draft); the other, which was published in the first, Paris edition of the symphony, is in 3/4. It was long supposed that the 6/8 movement, being the longer and the more elaborate (though neither could be said to have 'too much modulation'), was the original and the 3/4 the replacement. But doubt has been cast on this, particularly by the discovery of a sketch sheet which on one side contains a working of a few bars for the finale and on the other the melodic outline of the 3/4 movement. Still, we do not know which side he used first; and the fact that he left the 3/4 movement to be published in Paris but took the 6/8 one home (revising it during the journey) may seem to argue in favour of the traditional view. It is also worth noting that in its draft form the 6/8 movement was even longer, which would seem unlikely for a movement intended as a shorter substitute. The replacement movement was performed in the symphony at the Feast of the Assumption concert on 15 August. The Paris publication said on the title-page 'Du Repertoire du Concert Spirituel'.

Whichever movement came first, there is no doubt that the 6/8 one is the superior for its graceful lines and its warmth of expression. It is in sonata form, without development and with a final, partial reminder of the main theme. Mozart's draft suggests that he originally had in mind to make it a sonata-rondo, with a long minor-key episode, but he must have realised that this would make it far too long. One other notable detail of his revision concerns a point in the second-subject material, where a two-bar phrase is expressively echoed in the minor. In the recapitulation he wrote just the same, but then he reversed it, so that the minor-key pair of bars came first with a major echo: the emotional effect is quite different, with balm after the hint of sadness.

The 3/4 Andante is far simpler, much in the manner of a serenade slow movement. It is planned on a miniature scale: the opening theme –

which never recurs – reaches the dominant key within eight bars, and after a four-bar link the second subject (another eight bars) ensues, with a six-bar closing section. After ten bars' development, the material from the link onwards is recapitulated, with the ending slightly expanded. The music has an air of elegant sensibility rather than expressiveness. Curiously, the three-octave string texture we met in the first movement appears again here, this time with the cellos additionally involved; their music, exceptionally for Mozart, is often different from that for the double-basses. Another unusual feature of the scoring is the use of only a single flute and oboe among the upper woodwind.

There is no minuet; Parisian symphonies rarely have them. The finale here is a helter-skelter, dashing affair designed to show off the Paris violins and to surprise and delight the audience – especially, as we saw, with its hushed beginning. For all the surface brilliance, however, it is a well-proportioned and well-argued example of sonata form, with a development that, picking up a phrase used earlier to steer the music into the second subject, has a lively fugal development and a suitably dazzling coda. Counterpoint need not, Mozart shows, be learned or academic. But one Parisian critic, writing of a performance a year later, had reservations about it: 'We noticed in the first two movements a strong character, a great richness of idea and some well-developed motifs. As to the third, where the entire science of counterpoint shone forth, it gained the approbation of the lovers of a kind of music that can engage the mind without ever touching the heart.'

In a letter home, Mozart talked of his 'two' Paris symphonies, implying, though without actually saying directly, that both were new. Commentators have exerted themselves to find a second (some have even imagined they had found it, in the unbelievably feeble two-movement piece K.311a/C11.05, which for a brief while was permitted to intrude into the Köchel numeration); but it seems clear, on reading between the lines of Mozart's letters, that any second must have been an older work he had brought with him.

Mozart's next symphonies, then, belong to his final years in Salzburg, 1779–80, when he occupied a *Konzertmeister* post, officiating as court organist. The likelihood is that these three symphonies were written for use at the Salzburg court. The first, No. 32 in G, K.318, has often been suspected of having theatrical origins, mainly because it is in one continuous movement, though it does not in fact follow the traditional Italian opera-overture pattern. It has been coupled tentatively with Mozart's music for *Thamos, König in Ägypten* and, with unwonted assurance, with his unfinished Singspiel known as *Zaide*. The date, April 1779, does not quite match either possibility; it is however conceivable that Mozart intended it for use in some kind of theatre production by the travelling troupe of J. H. Böhm, with whom he was then in contact and who was planning a visit to Salzburg. Several years later, in Vienna, the work was used as overture to an opera, *La villanella rapita* by Francesco Bianchi, for which Mozart also provided two vocal numbers.

Its theatricality is not only a matter of its form. Written for a large orchestra – pairs of flutes, oboes, bassoons and trumpets, with four horns (two each in G and D) and timpani, besides the strings – it starts with a rhetorical, gesture-like phrase (Ex. 17), whose upward swoop and falling octave serve as a motif. There are sharp contrasts of loud and soft, striding arpeggios and a virile bass-line. When the music comes to a halt, ready to restart in the new key, Mozart, instead of continuing with the secondary theme, first gives the whole orchestra a unison, accented semibreve D, a powerfully arresting gesture. The theme itelf is of a marked *opera buffa* character; but when it finishes there follows a typical 'Mannheim crescendo' – a protracted one, with tremolando strings, and the rest of the orchestra gradually coming in, all above a repeated-note bass: exactly along the model favoured at Mannheim. The development, beginning in relaxed fashion, moves into an emphatic tutti containing, in the inner strings, a dialogue on the motif in Ex. 17. The music seems to be leading back to a recapitulation, but suddenly breaks off for a gentle 3/8 Andante, a movement within a movement (it is a miniature sonata-rondo, in G, with generous writing for the woodwind and horns). The Andante leads back to a 'Primo Tempo' marking, and the original Allegro spiritoso resumes with a brief tutti. The second subject follows, heralded as before by an accented unison; but at the very end Ex. 17 returns, with new dramatic force – and this time it takes an extra step, up to octaves on E, supported by brass in a fanfare rhythm and a roll from the timpani. The orchestra momentarily hushes, but normality returns and the work is rounded off by an eleven-bar tutti. That extraordinary moment, when the music steps beyond its expected frame, leaves its impact: it embodies a hint of alarming realities behind the façade of orderliness.

Ex.17

K318, i.1

If in No. 32 Mozart was showing his Salzburg friends (and enemies) what he had learnt in the wider world of Mannheim and Paris, in No. 33 in B♭, K319, he is thoroughly Austrian once again. This work, written in the summer of 1779, is for a more modest orchestra, just oboes, bassoons, horns and strings; and its opening bars, where divided violas support the violins, show that it is music in which refinement and finesse of colour play a part. The music is in 3/4 metre, and has something of the vitality usual in Mozart's triple-time music, especially in the tuttis, which additionally are distinguished by the ring of the horns pitched in high B♭. But string quartet-like textures appear a good deal, and in the main second-subject theme the woodwind provide delicate answering phrases. The material is subjected to a good deal of development within the exposition (one graceful phrase heard early on, in particular, is ingeniously used later in a quartet-like passage and, in the bass, in the tutti that follows); so it is not surprising that the 'development' itself is interludial, based wholly on two new motifs. One of these is a four-note figure (Ex. 18a), much used by Mozart, and quite often by other composers too, in contrapuntal contexts: Mozart's most famous use of it is in the finale of his last symphony, the 'Jupiter' (see pp. 96–100). In the present symphony, it runs through the main part of the development section, carrying the music from one key to another while counterpoints are woven around it. The recapitulation is straightforward, with a certain amount of extension to help the focus on the home key as well as some typically subtle changes of line occasioned by the different register that the new key requires; there is also a short coda, embodying a little extra development and a sudden, hushed moment of chromatic harmony, a shadow which quickly passes to make way for a lively ending.

Ex.18

(a) Allegro assai

K319, i.143

(b) Andante moderato

ii.44

iii.162

The Andante cleaves even more closely to the world of chamber music. In E♭, it has all the warmth traditional to that key (it is the usual one for the operatic *aria d'affetto*, the heroine's central expression of feeling). It is in sonata form, with a reversed recapitulation, a pattern uncommon in a slow movement; it works well, however, providing a strong sense of homecoming and finality conjoined. Its 'development', once again, is on fresh material: but is it really quite fresh? Ex. 18*b*, used (like Ex. 18*a* in the first movement) in imitation between voices, has in fact the same note-pattern as Ex. 18*a* but with an octave displacement (as Ex. 18*c* shows); this could be mere coincidence, but there is no special reason to think that something apparent to a twentieth-century student of Mozart's music would not have been very much more so to Mozart himself when composing it.

What is even more curious, however, is that at exactly the same juncture in the finale another linked 'new' idea appears: with one note altered (C to G), Ex. 18*d* would exactly match *a* and *b*, and it too is used with counterpoints woven around it as the basis of a development section. The rest of the movement, a charming and beautifully-shaped frolic, is almost wholly innocent of counterpoint, being made up of scurrying triplets, an answering theme in a more graceful but still jig-like dotted rhythm, and, after a witty linking passage, a main second-subject theme which while glancing at the world of *opera buffa* retains the chamber-musical sophistication that marks this particular symphony – though that is soon put aside with the perky little march with which the oboes and bassoons round out the exposition. This symphony was originally composed in three movements. Reviving it in Vienna a few years later, Mozart added a cheerful minuet to meet the Viennese taste; in the shapely lines of its trio especially, Mozart recaptured the work's unique expressive world.

Within four weeks of completing Symphony No. 33, Mozart had

written the last of his big Salzburg serenades, the one known as the 'Posthorn', K.320. This work and its 1776 predecessor, the 'Haffner', K.250/248b, come close to the realms of the symphonies in their flanking movements (the first and the last three: the movements in between are mostly of the concerto type). Without actually belonging to the canon – for there are important differences in their style and expressive ambience – these works nevertheless occupy a significant role in Mozart's development as an orchestral composer and in particular in his capacity for handling expansive sonata-form movements: no study of the symphonies would be complete without mention of them, particularly as Mozart himself used them as symphonies on occasion.

It was a further year before Mozart wrote his next symphony, No. 34 in C, K.338 – the last he was to compose in his native city. Probably the occasion for it was a group of concerts at the Salzburg court at the beginning of September 1780 in which he was involved. It immediately invokes the traditions of C major martial brilliance with its pompous opening, using triadic figures and fanfare rhythms, and its trumpet-and-drum textures, though the *piano* echoes of the *forte* phrases offer an early hint that this is more than merely martial music. One of the echo phrases touches on the minor mode, as too does the extended tutti that follows; and there are hints of shadows in the second-subject music too, where the bassoons (later the oboes) counterpoint the violin theme with a descending chromatic line, in enhanced imitation of a linking phrase just heard. A Mannheim crescendo leads into the powerful tutti – again embodying flirtations with the minor mode – that carries us towards the end of the exposition. The section that follows is again interludial, developing nothing but its own ideas. It is important not to regard this type as in any sense aesthetically inferior to the 'true' developments of a Haydn or a Beethoven simply because historical progress was to lie with the latter type. The composer's job was to create great art, not to map out the future. This particular example is apt, ingenious and attractive, especially its theatrical beginning where the music moves in an unexpected harmonic direction and then, still more unexpectedly, leads us almost epigrammatically into the Schubertian distant regions of Ab major. The music here – intentionally, of course – is almost void and characterless, simply a way of creating time-space so that the recapitulation can make its appointed effect. From Ab Mozart steers us gently through F minor to C minor, and on to the dominant of C major, the harmony ever slower-moving, teasing us a little in our eager expectation of arrival back in C major with the opening material. When it comes,

Mozart drops the echo passages we heard in the exposition and, with some development of the opening flourish, short-circuits the first tutti and hastens on to the second subject; and in the music that follows he again takes a short cut (the Mannheim crescendo is omitted) but substantially increases the drama of the ensuing tutti with his reshaping of the line and the harmony. And at the point parallel to the end of the exposition he brings back the very opening music – this time complete with its echoes – to round off the movement with a final blaze of C major martial fanfaring.

Mozart next wrote a minuet, but at some stage decided to exclude it; he tore out of the score most of the pages on which it was written, but of course had to leave the opening since it was on the back of the ending of the first movement. Its fourteen struck-out bars show a pleasant but unexceptional piece. It has been suggested that the minuet K.409/383f, written in Vienna some three years later, was intended for use in the symphony when Mozart performed it in the capital, but the piece is far too long and poorly matched to the symphony in style and in the orchestra it requires; there are no grounds for performing it with the rest of the work.

Mozart marked the slow movement 'Andante di molto', which might be thought to indicate a speed on the slow side of plain Andante; but for a copy he made later (this was one of a group of symphonies he sold to the music-loving Prince von Fürstenberg) he added 'più tosto allegretto', implying the opposite. Scored only for strings, with bassoons adding definition to the bass-line and the violas divided to permit a richer texture, it is in the tradition of those movements we noted earlier consisting of an unbroken, or nearly unbroken, line of melody. It is music of warm and delicate sensibility rather than of emotional depth, and is carefully composed, with many subtle differences when phrases are repeated; of these the most obvious is at the beginning where the principal theme, after reaching a half-close, is assigned to the second violins while the firsts add a counterpoint above. Although the textures are highly refined in their detail, the music's expressive character remains distinctively that of orchestral rather than chamber music.

The finale, marked (like the first movement) Allegro vivace, is his last and most brilliant in the much-favoured 6/8 metre. Its principal theme is a dashing scale-passage for the orchestra in unison; secondary ones include a spirited little idea for the violins which, typically of Mozart's mature orchestral writing, is repeated with a gloss for the oboes, and a rollicking phrase for the oboes answered by the whole orchestra.

Immediately after that is a tutti whose busy bass-line is at once taken up, *piano*, by the violins. The development, taking the oboe theme as its starting-point, has its moments of harmonic drama, but before long is gently but firmly guided back to C major and an orthodox recapitulation by the woodwind. The vigour and the substantial scale of this symphony make it a candidate – another, perhaps even stronger, is the Paris – for identification as the symphony which, Mozart told his father, went 'magnifique' at a concert in Vienna in April 1781, with forty violins, ten violas, eight cellos, ten double-basses, six bassoons and all the other wind doubled. We do well to remember that modestly-scaled performances are not the whole story of authenticity.

Vienna, 1782–6

In 1781, Mozart finally broke with the Salzburg court. At the beginning of the year he had enjoyed a success at Munich with his 'grand opera' *Idomeneo*, and then had been summoned to Vienna to provide music for the Salzburg archbishop, who was on a state visit to the imperial capital. Seeing the opportunities open to him there, and chafing at the Salzburg bit, on which the archbishop was tugging severely, he eventually obtained his dismissal.

Mozart had no regular employment in Vienna, at least until 1787; he made his living by teaching, by giving concerts, privately and (occasionally) in public, by writing operas, by composing for publication – and any other way he could. His reputation in Vienna was essentially as a pianist, as it had been since his earliest visits as a child. And Vienna, as he wrote in a letter home, was 'the land of the piano'. His early publications there were sonatas for piano, with and without violin, and piano concertos. At his public concerts, he shone above all by playing, in concertos and solo works; if he needed a symphony, he had some good recent ones to draw on. In fact, he wrote no symphony with Viennese performance in mind until 1788.

The stimulus for his next symphony came from Salzburg. During the summer of 1782 he had a letter from his father asking him to write a symphony for the celebrations in Salzburg on the ennoblement of Siegmund Haffner, a member of a leading local family with whom the Mozarts were on friendly terms; his Haffner Serenade of 1776 had been written on the occasion of a wedding in the family. He responded:

> At the moment I'm not exactly short of work. – By Sunday week I have to arrange my opera for wind band – otherwise someone else will get in ahead of me – and deprive me of the profits; and now you ask me to write a new symphony! – it's hardly possible! . . . Well, I shall have to work at it during the nights, there's nothing else to be done – for your sake, dearest father, I make the sacrifice. – You may rely on receiving something every post-day – and I shall work just as fast as I can – and as far as haste permits – I shall write a good piece.

The new opera was *Die Entführung aus dem Serail*, which had had its première four days earlier; Mozart did not in fact prepare the wind arrangement in time. He was on the point of moving house, and was to be married in two weeks. It is hardly surprising, then, that a week later he could send only the first movement (he apologised, explaining that he had also had to compose a wind serenade); 'on Wednesday the 31st', he added, 'I shall send the 2 minuets, the Andante and the last movement . . . I have written it in D as that is your favourite.' When 31 July came, the symphony remained unfinished:

> You can see that my intentions are good; but when something can't be done, it can't be done! – I'm not going to turn out rubbish. – So I'll be able to send you the whole symphony on the next post-day. – I could let you have the last movement now, but I'd rather send it all together, for a single postage fee.

He apparently sent the symphony, all together, during the next few days (he was incidentally married on the Sunday of that week, 4 August). The following week he wrote home again, enclosing a new march (probably K.408 No. 2/385a) to be used with the symphony, and saying: 'I only hope it will all reach you in good time – and will be to your taste. – The first Allegro must go with real fire – the last – as fast as possible.' Whether or not the music arrived in time we do not know; the actual date of Haffner's ennoblement was 29 July, but the celebrations may well have taken place later.

In December, with Viennese concerts in prospect, Mozart asked his father to send a copy of the symphony back to him. He renewed the request in January, asking too for several other symphonies – K.201, 182 and 183, and the symphony movements from the serenade K.204 (perhaps it may be inferred from this that he already had copies of more recent works, like K.338, 319, 318 and 297). After two more, increasingly pressing, reminders, Leopold sent the symphonies, to which Mozart responded: 'The new Haffner symphony was a total surprise to me – I hadn't remembered a thing about it; – it must surely make a good effect.'

He proceeded to make the effect even better. Written for a festive occasion in Salzburg, the symphony originally called for maximum Salzburg forces: pairs of oboes, bassoons, horns, trumpets and drums and strings. In Vienna, flutes and clarinets were available too – and we know that Mozart relished the enriched sound of a fuller wind group (see p. 54). The score had been written on the middle ten staves of 12-staff manuscript paper, leaving the top and bottom ones empty; Mozart now used the top one for a pair of flutes and the bottom for a pair of clarinets, though only in the outer movements. He took care to add the extra instruments only in the tuttis, and in such a way that no rewriting of the existing parts was necessary. (When, some years later, he added clarinets to No. 40 in G minor he gave them a much more prominent role and had to revise the oboe parts.) He also crossed through the double bar at the centre of the first movement, so eliminating the two repeats (in fact, he had not completed the indication of the second repeat in his original score, so his intention remains ambiguous). It is generally believed that he further omitted a minuet, but this must be doubtful. The sole evidence for the existence of a second minuet is the reference in Mozart's letter to sending '2 minuets'. Though the idea of a symphony with two minuets, one either side of the slow movement, is unknown, this was a fairly usual form in lighter works (it appears for example in the wind serenade K.375, probably written in 1781), and might not have been inappropriate to a symphony designed for a festive occasion. If another minuet existed, however, it is lost without trace; Mozart may well have meant, by '2 minuets', the minuet and trio, or he may in the event have decided to write only one. There is a further puzzle regarding the minuet (the known one) of this symphony. The manuscript paper on which Mozart wrote it happens to be of a different kind from that used for the rest of the work, and this has given rise to the idea that it may have been composed later, when Leopold returned the score, to replace the previous minuet or minuets – though it is perfectly possible that, when writing it, Mozart simply took his paper from a different pile (the movement fits exactly on a standard double sheet). And had he been composing a new minuet at the time when he was adding extra instruments to the outer movements he would surely have incorporated parts for them in it.

The Haffner Symphony, No. 35 in D, K.385, had its first Viennese performance at Mozart's 'academy' (or concert) in the Burgtheater on 23 March. Emperor Joseph II was present and, according to Mozart's report of the event, was 'delighted beyond all bounds'. It was a long programme: Mozart played two piano concertos, a fugue and two sets of variations, members of the orchestra played the concerto-style movements from his last Salzburg serenade, and four arias were sung. The symphony opened the programme and its finale closed it, although it is not clear whether the whole symphony or just the first three movements were played at the beginning.

For a symphony designed for serenade-like purposes, the Haffner is remarkably concentrated music. Its opening motif (Ex. 19a) pervades the whole first movement. It soon returns, to introduce the first tutti, at the end of which, *piano* in the violins and then *forte* in the basses, with the opposite group counterpointing it each time, it leads to the new key

– where, in the violas, it serves as counterpoint to a lyrical dialogue among the violins (Ex. 19*b*). Its octave leaps are now absent for a while, but its rhythm dominates the next tutti (Ex. 19*c*), and this form of it is echoed (Ex. 19*d*) in the *piano* passage that ensues. This kind of trans-

Ex.19

Allegro con spiritoso

(a)

K385, i.1

(b) violins

p (+ wind sustaining)

violas

i.48 (+ 8ve lower)

(c) (+ 8ve lower)

f

i.59

(d)

i.67

formation – modifying the shape and character of a theme almost beyond recognition, while its germinal role remains unmistakable – is less familiar in Mozart than in Beethoven and the high Romantics. Predictably, this motif dominates the development section, where it is used in various kinds of imitation; its scale pattern (as at one point in the exposition) moves upwards as well as downwards, and it readily carries the music through a number of keys and then decisively homewards to D major for the recapitulation. Particularly characteristic here is the first tutti, veering off towards G major, then returning with some emphatic violin writing while the motif strides down in the basses from G to A (the home dominant, to prepare for the return of Ex. 19*b*), while its martial rhythms occupy the brass and timpani.

If the first movement's close organisation places it nearer to the world of the symphony than that of the serenade, in the Andante the flowing and gracefully ornamental melody and the gentle hints of pathos (like the accented chromatic comments from the oboe and the bassoon – not far distant from Pamina's world in *Die Zauberflöte*) recall the serenade atmosphere more clearly, as too does the delicacy of the string scoring in the second subject. The movement is in straightforward sonata form, each half repeated, with a 'development' of the marking-time type. The minuet and trio, cast entirely in four-bar phrases (very unusual for Mozart, except in real dance music), are close too to the serenade manner, the one pompously festive, the other unpretentiously lyrical.

The finale, even if 'to be played as fast as possible', and enormously high-spirited, is no mere frolic. Its music is closely organised. Its main theme, a near relative (as is often pointed out) of Osmin's 'Ha! wie will ich triumphiren' from *Die Entführung*, with its falling triad pattern and its semitone inflection (Ex. 20*a*, *x* and *y*), gives rise to the bass of the tutti (Ex. 20*b*), which is taken up by the violins and becomes the movement's main propellant motif. This is another of those movements whose broad structure is *sui generis*, basically sonata form but with

69

Ex.20

(a)

K385, iv.1

(b)

iv.9

features that incline it towards rondo. It has a conventional exposition, with clear first and second subjects. Then the opening music returns, but soon swerves off into B minor, where the second subject now reappears. Before long we are back to normal with the recapitulation. This can, of course, be construed simply as a development section where the first subject makes an appearance in the home key (and this is by no means unique: it often happens in pre-classical music, and in Haydn's works of all periods). But the formal ambiguity is retrospectively reinforced when, at the end of the recapitulation, after a witty little link, Mozart embarks on the first subject all over again. This time, however, and with a delicious elegance, he soon diverts it from its earlier course to provide a firm sense of finality.

In the summer of 1783, Mozart took Constanze, his new wife, to Salzburg to meet his father and sister. On the return journey, in the autumn, they travelled through Linz, where Mozart was entertained by a leading local figure, Count Thun. He wrote home on 31 October: 'On Tuesday 4 November I am giving an academy in the theatre here, – and as I haven't a single symphony by me I am writing a new one at breakneck speed, which must be ready by then.'

Mozart's Linz Symphony, No. 36 in C, K.425, is his first to begin with a slow introduction. He had used introductions before only in a couple of serenade-type pieces, though later, among the larger-scale works of his maturity, he was to do so more often. In this, as in many features of his style, he was a creature of his times. Haydn too had written only a modest number of slow introductions in his eighty-odd symphonies to date (fewer than a dozen; most recently in Nos. 71, 73 and 75, all from around 1779–82), but was to do so increasingly in the years to come. Possibly Mozart had the idea from Haydn (we know, from the fact that he jotted down its opening bars on a piece of manuscript paper dating from 1782–3, that he was acquainted with No. 75), or from his gifted younger brother Michael, a Salzburg colleague and friend. This introduction starts with a fanfare-like figure, in sharply dotted rhythms that recall the arresting character of the French overture; softer music, chromatically tinged, follows, with a figure heard on the bassoon and the oboe taken down into the basses, when the harmonic movement slows down and becomes repetitive, heightening our expectation for the main Allegro.

This is a splendid, broad, expansive piece, with a touch of the traditional C major ceremonial character (there are trumpets and drums in the orchestra), and unusually clear-cut in design. Mozart's haste over the writing of it finds no apparent reflection in the music itself. The opening theme consists of a four-bar phrase (Ex. 21a; note the little upward flick, x) answered by a six-bar one; the tutti that follows repeats, *forte*, the four-bar phrase, converting its last bar into four bars by insistent repetition, and then varies the six-bar one, giving it a lyrical turn to cadence in C major and a bright, noisy tutti, with the basses sawing away and the brass stressing Mozart's favourite martial rhythm. This leads to the dominant key, G, where the music quietens and, with a phrase using the upward flick we heard earlier, reaches a cadence. The main second-subject idea, which follows, is an emphatic statement of E minor, gently diverted back to G major; repeated, it is a gentle statement of E minor, emphatically diverted back, and fixed there by a finely sonorous and brilliant tutti. It is worth noting that each time the tutti breaks off (and this applies equally to the echoes after it) the final notes, Ex. 21b, recall the end of the opening phrase of the movement, Ex. 21a: another example of Mozart's altering a theme while retaining

Ex.21

K425, i.20

i.104

its identity as a means of holding the music together. The brief development is concerned almost wholly with the idea heard on the violins at the end of the tutti, and the recapitulation closely follows the exposition; that might be taken as symptomatic of Mozart's haste in composition, although this work is far from the only one with such features, as we have seen. The short coda is based on the idea used in the development.

The slow movement, marked Poco Adagio – and thus a significant departure from the usual Andante – inaugurates a series of symphony slow movements of a new seriousness and depth of feeling. This is immediately clear in the dense, almost brooding quality of sound in the first tutti, a *piano* one, which follows the first four bars of the principal theme. Here we have the first violins in a middle–high register, carrying the melodic line, the seconds in an 'Alberti' pattern on their G and D strings, the violas sustaining in the same register, the basses pizzicato, while all the wind, including trumpets, also sustain, with the horns pursuing the violin line. If it is unusual for the trumpets to be given a voice in a slow movement, to which, predominantly playing *piano*, they bring a certain hieratic solemnity, it is at least equally so for the timpani, whose gentle thuds further darken the sound. This texture is worth describing in full as, with various modifications, it becomes an important part of Mozart's expressive armoury in the slow movements of his late symphonies. A variety of it appears, made more sinister by a turn to the minor, in the second subject, whose principal theme is made up of brief phrases each of which seems to resolve the one before but needs to be resolved itself. In one, the pleas of Gluck's Orpheus to the Furies are suggested by the alternation of stern wind chords and pleading phrases on the violins. The main event of the development is the appearance of a new idea, not of the usual kind for such contexts (most commonly lyrical or motivic) but consisting mainly of a rising staccato scale, on the bassoon, cellos and double-basses, then taken up, and taken over, by the violins, who extend it and (when it returns to the bass regions) counterpoint it. Something quite similar happens in a symphony by Michael Haydn which Mozart knew, and which we shall shortly meet again; perhaps that was the idea's source. But soon the recapitulation arrives, its expression now intensified – by the elaboration of the melodic line, by the climactic moment where the violins reach chromatically upward only to fall away again, and in the intensely chromatic music at the cadence for oboes and bassoon, now still more poignant than earlier. And the movement ends to the grave, disturbing sound of a wind group with trumpets and drums playing softly.

But the minuet is cheerful, open C major music, full of military pomp in its main section, which neatly bows itself out with an epigrammatic phrase echoing the beginning of the movement. The trio is in the manner of that favourite Austrian folkdance, the *Ländler*, an easygoing predecessor of the waltz beloved of Schubert, Bruckner and Mahler; this charming example is intended for more elegant folk, with its sophisticated oboe and bassoon, then both (even in imitation), doubling the violins. It is an excellent foil to the heartiness of the main part of the minuet.

The finale of the Linz Symphony has good claims to be counted Mozart's wittiest instrumental piece. It has a plethora of ideas, all of them quite short and lightly contrasted with one another; however, their family resemblance, as it were, is unmistakable, and may perhaps be put down to certain common features – notably the rising fourth of the opening, which is present in virtually all of them in some guise, and the dotted rhythm, also heard at the opening. The main idea of the second subject stresses the fourth in particular, with a sharp accent, but the pattern is broken with its continuation, which one could reasonably call a double fugue if that did not sound absurdly pompous for such relaxed, entertaining, easygoing music. But the themes (or figures) concerned do in fact pass orthodoxly from one voice to another – if more like the relay-runner's baton than serious musical dialectic. At the climax, however, the violins bring in a new and more serious idea (compare bars 48ff in the first movement), partly in counterpoint to the 'fugue subject', to guide the music, with some chromatic and minor-key inflections, to a cadence. There the fun starts again, with a scurrying theme (another relative of the family we met before) and a *moto perpetuo* one, leading to a *fortissimo* development of the opening idea to crown the exposition. The development itself is built wholly around a broken-chord theme, originally heard in the first tutti of the movement. Now it gives rise to a noisy tutti, where the bass instruments chase the violins up and down its broken-chord patterns; then it is passed – the relay race again – from one instrument to another, bassoon, oboe and strings, while the music works its way home to C major and, of course, the recapitulation. This, as before a possible sign of Mozart's haste, is again unusually regular, though not without a characteristic twist or two of register and an appealing touch of chromaticism at the point where the music diverges from the exposition; and the final tutti is extended and given extra emphasis.

When Mozart wrote from Linz that he had no symphony by him, he presumably meant no symphony of his own. He may well have had a symphony, perhaps two, by Michael Haydn. One of these, a G major work (No. 18 in the Perger catalogue of Michael Haydn's symphonies), was long thought to be Mozart's own. Early students of Mozart's music took it to be his Linz symphony; Köchel gave it the number 444, and the editors of the nineteenth-century complete works included it as Symphony No. 37. These notions were derived from the fact that there exists a manuscript of the symphony of which the first half is in Mozart's hand. When, early this century, the work was firmly identified as by Michael Haydn, and was known to have been composed in 1783, it was very reasonably supposed that Mozart had brought it back with him from Salzburg to Vienna and used it en route at his Linz academy. The symphony as composed by Michael Haydn begins with an Allegro con spirito; Mozart, apparently feeling that the opening was a shade per-emptory, added an Adagio maestoso introduction. This, it was long assumed, was done at Linz (hence the revised Köchel number, 425a); but research on the types of paper Mozart used shows that the introduc-tion is likelier to have been written in Vienna, late in 1783 or early in 1784. Probably he used the symphony in one of the academies he gave during the spring of 1784, when he was at the height of his success as a concert-pianist; it is entirely in accordance with the outlook of the times that, if one composer thought that another's symphony could be improved, he would carry out the improvement himself.

Three years passed – years that saw the composition of a dozen piano concertos, *Le nozze di Figaro* and much chamber music – before Mozart wrote another symphony. On 6 December 1786, according to the thematic catalogue of his works that he had kept since early 1784, he completed a symphony in D. Mozart had planned a series of Advent concerts in Vienna at around this time, but we do not know whether they took place; it may be that the Piano Concerto in C K.503 and this symphony (K.504) were composed with these concerts in prospect. Viennese symphonies, however, normally had four movements, includ-ing a minuet, and the fact that this one is in only three may imply that it was intended for elsewhere. All we know for certain, however, is that Mozart went to Prague early in January 1787 and that Symphony No. 38 in D, known as the Prague Symphony, had a performance (very likely its first) in the theatre there on 19 January.

Mozart liked Prague, and Prague liked Mozart. This was the first of his four visits to the Bohemian capital, and was wholly happy. He found himself a celebrity there, more than he ever had been in Vienna: *Figaro* had enjoyed unprecedented success, and (as he reported in a letter to a friend) the whole city was dancing to its tunes – 'nothing is played, sung or whistled but *Figaro*'. On the strength of its success he was invited to write a new opera for production in the city: this was to be *Don Giovanni*.

The Prague Symphony has often been said to foreshadow the Prague opera, especially in its slow introduction. This, much more extended than the one in the Linz, or indeed than most of Haydn's, gives a clear sense of the scale of the work to come. Like the Linz's, it starts with an arresting gesture, then moves to softer music. But that is not all, for there follows a sequence of alternate *forte* and *piano* bars, as if compressing the conflict of loud and soft, or dark and light, or severe and gentle, while the music is guided from D minor through B flat to, eventually, the dominant of the main key, D. The harmony, as usual at such a juncture, becomes repetitive, and the level fades to a *pianissimo* – but the heavy texture and in particular the presence of quiet trumpets and drums leave no room for doubt about the *gravitas* or the scale of the work.

Nor indeed does the opening of the Allegro, which uniquely marries the traditions of D major festive brilliance with serious symphonic argument of a kind that we have seen gradually develop in Mozart's music (it does so too, rather differently, in Haydn's). The main theme of the movement is at first hearing a shade uninteresting in itself (Ex. 22*a*), yet clearly it is full of ideas that promise some kind of development. The bars immediately following show this, with the figure y^2 used to accompany a continuation in the first violins (Ex. 22*b*), while the shape of x is, literally, reflected in the main figure (Ex. 22*c*) of the tutti that ensues. After that tutti we are in the dominant key and expecting a new, second-subject idea: but what comes is a revised version of the first, with a new chromatic inflection (Ex. 22*d*, the notes marked ×: in a surviving sketch, the Es are unsharpened, so evidently the inflection was a late idea) and a continuation that builds a contrapuntal argument from y^1 in Ex. 22*a* and the first-violin figure from Ex. 22*b*, giving rise to a fiery tutti. This is closely akin to Haydn's technique of using the main first-subject idea, often with a different (and usually contrapuntal) continuation, for his second subject. Other composers did the same: it was a natural and effective way of holding together the structure of a large-scale movement. But for Mozart the element of lyrical contrast was not readily to be foregone, and after the tutti a new theme is presented by the first violins, with echoes on the bassoons when it dips into the minor

(d) (strings)

i.71

key – and when the violins move on to a new continuation the bassoons
go on burbling away with the theme's opening phrase. One element in
this theme, and especially in its continuation, a simple four-note
descending scale (the first note sometimes tied over), hints at a link, to
be clarified later, with z from Ex. 22*a*. But for the moment Mozart
returns to the tutti based on Ex. 22*c*, reserving however for its climax – here
as in several other symphonies returning at this point in the exposition to
unmistakable first-subject material – x from Ex. 22*a*, now given maximum
prominence at the top of the texture instead of the bottom.

With so much development in the exposition, what is to happen
now? An interludial 'development'? That is what, at first, it seems like,
as the violins disport themselves in dialogue – but the matter of the
dialogue is in fact z from Ex. 22*a*. And now Mozart sets other ideas in
counterpoint against it, as the dialogue continues, more forcefully, with
the wind instruments adding their voices: figure y and Ex. 22*c* play a
prominent part, and eventually the latter prevails, pushing the music
rapidly through a series of keys, overshooting the home key of D major
but coming back to it, in a way that suggests a re-entry to the exposition
in its first tutti. But that is a deception. What ought, at the end of the
tutti, to have been the second subject (that is, the inflected version of the
first) in D major turns out to be at the pitch of A major; yet, curiously,
the key is clearly D nevertheless – and it quickly moves to D minor. It is
obvious that we are not after all recapitulating yet. The bass instruments
settle on an A, and it becomes plain that this static harmony is to herald
the recapitulation proper; above it, the violins are involved in four-note
descending scales (this time related more obviously to the lyrical
second-subject theme, their legato character makes clear), and they lead
gently towards D for the recapitulation.

But that too is not quite so simple. For Mozart, having used this
syncopated idea (Ex. 22*a*) so many times, could hardly have committed
the solecism of presenting it twice more at this stage, especially as we

have just heard most of the tutti that might be expected to follow the first appearance. So he elides the first- and second-subject versions of Ex. 22*a*, incorporating the chromatic inflection of the second subject but also figure *z* of the first. And then, as in so many recapitulations, he modulates far afield (G major and minor, B♭ major, D minor) – taking the opportunity for a poetic, hushed moment as first the oboe and then the woodwind as a group guide the changes of key – and so reinforces the home tonic on arrival there. The end of the tutti is given further force by Mozart's avoidance of a simple repeat of the violin scale phrase heard in the exposition; as so often, he makes a virtue of necessity, finding new and more pointed phrases as substitutes for music that would anyway have sounded poorly in the register required by the new key – and here the ensuing climax, too, is given a sharper melodic profile to carry through this more dramatic treatment. The lyrical second-subject music appears as before, excepting only some register changes of the kind with which Mozart so often makes his recapitulations more, expressively speaking, than mere copies of what has already gone. The same happens with the movement's final climax, at the point where in the exposition Mozart brought back the first-subject material: he does so again, but counterpoints it with a new line on the first violins, straining at the very top of their compass, makes the harmony more strikingly chromatic, and then repeats the six bars concerned with a different orchestral layout. The result is one of the greatest climaxes of all symphonic music, worthy of the remarkable movement that it crowns.

The scoring of this movement, and especially its tuttis, seems to predicate a large orchestra: the more surprising, then, that the standard for the Prague orchestra at this time was at most fourteen string players (besides pairs of flutes, oboes, bassoons, horns, trumpets and timpani). The Andante, naturally more intimate in mood, would seem better suited to a band of modest size. In 6/8 metre, it is straightforward in design, but so devised as to make much use of simple motifs in a variety of expressive contexts. The development, starting off with the gently pastoral music that serves to close the exposition, is made up mainly of the opening theme, heard rising from C major through D minor and E minor, before dialogue on the main, five-note motif takes over. In the recapitulation the first-subject material is, accordingly, somewhat compressed (and also, at first, decorated, as it had been in the development); but the second-subject music is recapitulated almost exactly (a brief diversion into the minor key is worth noting, especially in the light of the Paris Symphony 6/8 slow movement), and the five-note motif supplies an epigrammatic ending.

Like that of the Paris Symphony the finale, marked Presto, is clearly intended to be played 'as fast as possible'. (There is in fact some evidence, speculatively derived from analysis of the types of paper Mozart used, that this movement may have been the first he composed, possibly as a new finale for the Paris Symphony, to be given in Prague; it should however be added that there is no precedent in the mature Mozart for a substitution of this kind.) It is largely built around a four-note motif – identical with the first four notes of the duettino for Susanna and Cherubino in Act 2 of *Figaro*, where the latter escapes the enraged Count – which propels all the tuttis, recurs (after a well-defined second-subject theme, in dialogue between strings and woodwind) at the end of the exposition, and dominates the development. There it is heard at first from flute and oboes between weighty orchestral chords, but then provokes a driving contrapuntal section, with strings and woodwind in austere two-part writing. Mozart curiously tucks the beginning of the recapitulation into what seems like a continuing development (which is another, and in this case more appropriate, way of saying that the recapitulation is interrupted by further development). But once back to the second subject, the music follows a predictable course to its end, and in spite of the hints of darkness and even anger in the middle of the movement, there is no doubting that, by the time it finishes, wit and high spirits are firmly in the ascendant.

Vienna, 1788

It was not until the late spring of 1788 that Mozart turned again to the symphony. Three entries in his thematic catalogue tell the story: a symphony in E♭ was entered for (and quite possibly completed on) 26 June (No. 39, K.543); one in G minor for 25 July (No. 40, K.550); and one in C major for 10 August (No. 41, K.551). As we have no certain knowledge of any occasion or occasions for which these symphonies were composed, romanticists have been tempted into wondering whether Mozart may have written them out of some kind of inner compulsion. The idea is more appealing in that they represent his final symphonic utterance (though he was not, of course, aware of that at the time). But such a notion is totally alien to the late eighteenth century. It would have been unthinkable for Mozart or any of his contemporaries to embark on the arduous and time-consuming business of composing three substantial symphonies without some immediate, specific professional goal in view.

The documentation of Viennese concert life during this period is extremely scanty. All we have is a haphazard collection of programmes that have survived and are now in a Viennese library. But we do know, from a remark of Mozart's in a letter to his brother mason, Michael Puchberg, in June 1788, that he was planning a series of concerts to begin during that month or early in July. There is no evidence that these concerts actually took place. Were Mozart contemplating them, however, he would surely have prepared himself by writing some new works. One might have expected piano concertos; but the falling-off in his output in that genre (half a dozen in 1784, three each in 1785 and 1786, none in 1787 and only an isolated one in 1788) can only reflect a decreased interest in him as pianist–composer among Viennese audiences. Perhaps – and here Haydn's recent success as a symphonist in Paris, and the subsequent publication of his Paris symphonies (Nos. 82–87) in Vienna, could have played a part – he was interested in appearing before Viennese audiences in a different capacity.

Even if none of the new symphonies was heard in Vienna during the summer of 1788, there can be little doubt that Mozart performed them on other occasions; the notion that he died without ever hearing them is sentimental and wholly fanciful. During his 1789 tour, when he went as far afield as Berlin, he gave concerts not only in the Prussian capital but also in Dresden and Leipzig; the Leipzig event included at least one symphony, and the others almost certainly did so too. The following year, when he went to Frankfurt on the occasion of Leopold II's coronation as Holy Roman Emperor, he gave a concert there which was to have included two symphonies – though a contemporary report relates that only a familiar one was played and the other had to be cancelled as the concert overran. In 1791, a symphony by Mozart opened the spring charity concert of the Tonkünstler-Sozietät of Vienna; the conductor was Antonio Salieri, and the orchestra included the Stadler brothers, clarinettists, who were friends of Mozart's. These are the only occasions we specifically know of on which symphonies from among Mozart's last three might have been performed; probably there were several more.

Writers have often referred to Mozart's last three symphonies as a trilogy or a triptych. This too is a little fanciful, although there are senses, as we shall see, in which they could be regarded as complementary. To anyone conversant with the music publishing habits of the time, the decision to write three symphonies, as opposed to two or four, suggests that Mozart had publication in mind. It was customary, and convenient, for publishers to package works in sets – six for those on a moderate scale, three for larger ones. During these years Mozart was often (though by no means always) short of money; the summer of 1788 was one of his worst spells. Several of his works from around this time were clearly intended to produce ready cash through quick sale to a publisher. The symphonies were not in fact printed until after his death – a composer often held works back from publication for a time so that he could sell manuscript copies to patrons, and so that the impact of his first few performances would not be blunted by the music's familiarity; the paucity of Viennese performances of the symphonies could well have induced Mozart to delay.

We have seen, throughout this book, how close are the links between the key of a work and the nature of its expression. This is largely a matter of, in the widest sense, acoustical factors from which traditions developed – the different capacities of instruments and the relationships between them in different keys, the effects of the various temperaments used (equal temperament was by no means the rule in Mozart's time), and so on. The keys Mozart chose for his last three symphonies are all ones with strong associations in his music: C major, as we have repeatedly seen, with a ceremonious, often martial, trumpets-and-drums manner; Eb with lyrical warmth and richness of sonority, sometimes with a certain formality and grandeur; and G minor, like all the minor keys, with urgency and drama, perhaps also pathos. Mozart's selection of these particular keys for a group of three symphonies –

bearing in mind that the preceding symphony had been in D, another key with strong associations – is especially interesting in the light of his earlier pairings of works in G minor with others in E♭ (the piano quartets of 1785–6) and C major (the string quintets of 1787).

The E♭ symphony, No. 39, K.543, breaks new ground in its inclusion of clarinets in place of the usual oboes. Mozart had used clarinets in his symphonies before (the Paris and the Haffner), but almost exclusively to add richness to the tuttis; now, as in two of his piano concertos, K.482 in E♭ and K.488 in A, he makes them the central instruments of the woodwind ensemble, and what was still primarily a military-band instrument was required to take its place in the civilised dialogues of the concert-room.

The symphony has a slow introduction, beginning with a fanfare-like affirmation of the home key (in common with so many of Mozart's E♭ works: the K.132 symphony, the violin–viola sinfonia concertante, the two-piano concerto, the K.375 wind serenade, the piano and wind quintet, the K.482 piano concerto). This time the stern, arresting dotted rhythms have a hint of the atmosphere of the old French overture, heightened by the rat-a-tat of the timpani and the sound, as much sombre as festive, of the trumpets. The dotted rhythms take over, in an ostinato in the basses, while a sequence of harmonies – its outcome always predictable, but no less gripping for that – leads, against violin scales and flute arpeggios, to a firm establishment of the dominant and a more dramatic development, each group of violins striving to reach above the other, with the scales, now more sinisterly, in the basses. For once, Mozart does not keep us waiting on a dominant to begin the main part of the movement; rather, he gives us four mysterious, slow-moving chromatic bars that resolve painlessly and with satisfying, inescapable logic on to E♭ – and the Allegro gently enters.

The main theme of the movement strikes a note of intimacy quite unexpected in a symphony first movement, with its spare scoring and its graceful appoggiaturas; but for the echoes on horns and bassoons, it could be a string-quartet texture. More remarkable, its repeat is presented by the cellos and the double-basses; with the echoes now on the higher woodwind, and a counter-theme on the violins, it acquires a quite different perspective. In the tutti that ensues, the scales of the slow introduction reappear, in a new, more direct, sense. The tutti culminates in repeated statements of an emphatic figure, Ex. 23. The main second-subject theme is as unorthodox as the first, a lyrical dialogue between strings and woodwind, delicately scored, and all in

Ex.23

K543, i.89

two-bar phrases until Mozart breaks any excessive regularity by sneaking in a five-bar one. The closing tutti ends with a reminder of Ex. 23 – and this gives Mozart his lead into the development, for he uses it to shift first to G minor and then, more abruptly, to Ab. After a reminder, in this soft, warm-sounding key of the second subject, the Ex. 23 figure provides the basis of a dialogue between basses and violins, in C minor, which constitutes the main part of what is a rather brief development. One might have expected Mozart to compensate for this brevity with some diversions during the recapitulation; but in fact, apart from the customary changes of line occasioned by register differences, and one beguiling different violin phrase in the second subject (over almost too quickly to be taken in), the recapitulation is about as exact as one can be, until its final bars, which Mozart extends, and supports with brass fanfare figures, to provide a proper final emphasis.

The Andante, Mozart's only symphony movement in Ab, begins in gentle, idyllic fashion, with a long-breathed melody in two sections, each marked to be repeated; note how the opening phrase of the melody, in the basses, serves as starting-point for the second, so that the melody's continuation is in a sense its own counter-melody. This music is for strings only; then the wind blows, and clouds appear, with a turn to F minor – never a happy key – and one of those threatening textures of the kind we met in the Linz Symphony: the seconds and violas darkening it with their lower strings, the wind sustaining (though no trumpets this time), the first violins playing a jagged and impassioned line. When the music arrives in the dominant, the first part of the second subject is music we have already heard – the second phrase of the opening melody, but turned upside down, with the music heard earlier on the basses now on the woodwind and the violin counter-melody on the basses. The second limb of the second subject – reached after another passionate tutti, from which a lonely violin line winds upwards with chromatic notes that initially baffle the ear – is a simple phrase played in imitation by clarinets and bassoons. Again, it is not new: it was heard (with a trivial difference) from the flute at the first wind entry in the movement. This sensuously beautiful passage, almost foreshadowing the world of

Così fan tutte, seems to be repeating, but Mozart deftly turns it to steer the music back to A♭, and to the recapitulation – there has been so much development already that a development section as such, especially in so lyrical a movement, would have been inappropriate.

In any case, this time the recapitulation has a stream of surprises to offer, and the music becomes denser and richer in meaning. First, the wind take over the opening theme after four bars, allowing the violins to add a new counterpoint to it. Then, with the second phrase, the wind insert a series of downward scales, heightening the textural interest at a point where simple repetition might have seemed tautologous. At the beginning of the movement, the closing phrase of the first subject had glanced on the minor mode; this time the glance is taken seriously, and the music veers off, through an enharmonic modulation – A♭ to A♭ minor, G♯ minor to B major. And now the F minor tutti comes again, in B minor: nothing could be more violent than a semitone discrepancy from the expected key, B♭ minor. The music itself, too, is violent, modulating (by classical standards) wildly and unnervingly: from B minor through a moment of ambiguity to F major, D♭ major, A♭ minor and on to the dominant of the home key. The second-subject material is also elaborated: its first limb by the descending scale we had earlier, the lonely violin line by a poignantly expressive aspiration upwards and a dying fall. The imitative woodwind theme is again turned in a different direction when it promises to repeat, but again (this time guided by a mellifluous clarinet duo) leads back to the opening music. As in so many earlier symphony slow movements, this last appearance serves as coda, so lovingly handled with its falling, valedictory chromatic line, that it seems as if Mozart – all too understandably – was reluctant to bid it farewell.

The minuet, marked Allegretto, glances at the ballroom, with its sturdy gait and four-square rhythms; but its pomp and grandeur, and its busy violin writing, give off a properly symphonic air. Each of its halves is rounded off in graceful, almost exaggeratedly courtly fashion. In the trio, an idealised *Ländler*, Mozart exploits both registers of the clarinet – one instrument sings the melody in its most expressive cantabile voice (with echoes from the flute) while the other accompanies in its rich, oily 'chalumeau' region.

The E♭ symphony is sometimes said to be the most like Haydn of Mozart's last three. Resemblances to Haydn are in fact slender and superficial; it would be truer, perhaps, to call it the least unlike him. The finale is monothematic, like some of Haydn's, and it is witty; but there the similarities end. The wit of its opening theme is of a highly sophisticated kind, with nothing of Haydn's earthiness; and the extra stroke of ingenuity with which Mozart turns it from a first-subject theme into a second-, by making a monologue become a dialogue (see Ex. 24), is entirely his own. The idea of continuing it differently second time is admittedly one that often found favour with Haydn; but the poetic change of key that ensues – from B♭ major to F♯ minor – and the veiled orchestral texture with which Mozart sets off the expressive implications of this shift could belong to no one else. The theme is used in yet another, more chirpy version to close the exposition; and predictably, in view of its susceptibility to dialogue treatment, it runs through the entire development. Part of this development is remarkably like the first movement's, with dialogue between first violins and basses at a bar's distance, though here it becomes closer (the lower group chasing the upper at a half-bar) and more intense. But it is elegantly rounded off, with sustained harmonies on the clarinets and bassoons to guide the music back, after its visits to distant tonal regions, to E♭ major and the recapitulation. This is as exact as any Mozart wrote, like the first movement's, and has just the little padding out at the end that it needs for a due sense of finality – which Mozart promptly squanders by providing a mischievously epigrammatic ending.

Ex.24

No Mozart symphony has excited as much attention and comment as No. 40 in G minor, K.550. Views on it, however, have varied a good deal. Charles Rosen perhaps best represents that of the present day, writing of it as a work of 'passion, violence, and grief' and one 'of Mozart's supreme expressions of suffering and terror'. Schumann, however, thought of it as embodying nothing more than Hellenic grace; and Jack Westrup saw it as imbued with the spirit of *opera buffa*. Whether or not the creation of such a work as this should be linked with biographical circumstances is a difficult issue; many composers and other artists have produced tragic works in happy times and vice versa. Yet the production of a tragic work must at least presuppose the capacity to experience tragedy and transmute it. We may note that, at just the time when Mozart was at work on this symphony (at the end of June 1788), he wrote to his friend Puchberg, saying how much more readily he could compose in his new apartment away from the centre of Vienna: 'if . . . black thoughts did not come to me so often, thoughts that I banish with tremendous effort, things would be better still'. It is not unreasonable to see the G minor symphony as related to this troubled state of mind; though it would degrade the symphony to regard it as merely an expression of his personal suffering.

The link with *opera buffa* draws support from the identity of rhythm between the opening phrase of the symphony and Cherubino's aria 'Non so più, cosa son, cosa faccio', from *Figaro*; Mozart is in fact thought to have contemplated setting the aria in G minor at one stage. It would be wrong to make too much of this. The rhythms of the Italian language penetrate much of Mozart's invention, and, in this period, when Italian opera was heard from Lisbon to St Petersburg and London to Dresden, it affected most composers in some degree. But the curve of this opening theme, its reaching upward and its decline to a note lower than the one it started from, twice over, speaks eloquently to anyone with musical sensibilities and a feeling for the expressive language of the time. So too – for Mozart presses the message home – does the ensuing phrase, with its dying fall, and the pained wind chords with the strings' inexorable response. The world the symphony inhabits is established in these first twenty bars, and it is not contradicted when, as the opening is repeated, the second phrase is more optimistically pitched one degree higher rather than one lower, rising where earlier it had fallen and carrying the music into the major. The symphony exists, as Mozart did, in a stylised, conventional world, where the expression of emotion in art takes particular, accepted forms that make it coherent and meaningful to listeners. The G minor symphony may be an outburst, but only within well understood limits. How many of Mozart's listeners came to terms with the full significance of its utterance we can only guess: probably very few, for it seems that his musical language, so much more complex than anyone else's at the time, texturally and harmonically, was widely found bewildering in such works as this, or *Don Giovanni*, or some of the late chamber music. Indeed, the next generation too failed to come to terms with these works, since from Beethoven's time onwards the expression of strong emotion took forms altogether more overt and more violent. A century later still, Donald Tovey could say that Mozart's forms precluded 'scope for any music which by legitimate metaphor could be called tragic'. We may flatter ourselves in thinking that only with the increasing historical empathy of the later twentieth century has Mozart's expressive language come to be more fully understood.

The falling semitone figure that opens the symphony (Ex. 25*a*) – after three-quarters of a bar of a magical 'till-ready' figure, given a poetic, veiled colouring on the violas – puts its imprint on virtually all the thematic ideas of the first movement. The main second-subject theme, in dialogue between strings and woodwind, centres on falling semitones (Ex. 25*b*), and indeed stresses them in its continuation; and the music that leads to the close of the exposition uses them against the opening figure (which now, as we are in the major key, is a whole tone rather than a semi: in the recapitulation that will be restored). This passage (Ex. 25*c*), occurs twice, with the music exchanged, between high and low instruments, in both strings and woodwind; earlier, the second-subject theme had also undergone an exchange, with strings and woodwind assigned each other's music second time. This device, of repeating music with its colours, its registers or both inverted, puts the ideas in a subtly altered light and exploits their expressive potential the more richly. The idea is not new – we saw it, for example, in the first movement of the E♭ symphony; but it is used particularly often, and particularly effectively, here.

It is to appear again in the development, which however begins with an abrupt, disorientating (intentionally, of course) shift of key, to F♯ minor – very remote indeed from the home key, and the effect of remoteness is heightened as the music seems to slip, as if beyond control, through other keys. At the tutti, when it is briefly in E minor, the pattern of inversion returns: the basses have the opening theme, the violins a busy counterpoint to it, but a moment later (now in D minor) the violins play the theme and the basses the counterpoint. The tutti

Ex.25
(a)

K550, i.1

87

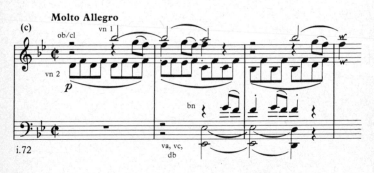

gives way to a series of dialogues on Ex. 25*a* between strings and woodwind, gradually drawing the music back towards G minor; when the key is re-established, an impassioned tutti presses it home, echoed (with emphasis on the falling line of the music) by woodwind – and the recapitulation steals in. There are still surprises to come. First, the little bassoon phrase that unobtrusively curls down as the opening theme has just begun, a sensitive reminder that the music cannot resume exactly as before: too much has happened for exact repetition to be tolerable. Then, where before the music moved to B♭, it now moves to E♭ – a standard recapitulation procedure in a major-key movement but not a minor-key one – and in a brief but fiery development of the three-note phrase that dominates this tutti Mozart turns the music back to the minor, as if forcing us to face a harsh reality. Once on to the second subject, the music is much as before, except in that the minor key darkens still further its utterance. Mozart, typically, strengthens the central cadence of the second subject by extending it, and at the very end there is a moment of threatened drama, from which, however, he seems to draw back, offering instead a few bars of imitation around the opening theme before the movement closes.

When Mozart embarked on the G minor symphony, he reverted to a more conventional orchestra: he dropped the clarinets of the E♭, restored the oboes, and did not call for trumpets (awkward to manage in G, still more in G minor) or drums. In his earlier G minor symphony, K.183/173dB, he had used two pairs of horns, one keyed in G and the other in B♭: this allowed him to use the horns most of the time in pairs and sometimes to enrich the texture considerably with horn tone. Here he used only two horns, one in G and one in B♭, in the outer movements, precluding much characteristic use of the instruments but still permitting him quite a lot of single horn notes even when the music was modulating a good deal. Later – it could have been for the 1791 Tonkünstler-Sozietät concerts, when (as we have seen) the Stadlers were present – he added clarinet parts, writing them out with revised oboe parts on a separate, amending series of pages. The clarinets are allotted most of the original oboe solos, though not all; they have a leading part, for example, in the main second-subject theme of the first movement in the exposition, but the oboes' sharper sound is preferred in the recapitulation when the same music is heard in the minor. The sustained notes traditionally belonging to the oboes in predominantly string passages remain their preserve.

The slow movement is a 6/8 Andante, not the Adagio one might have expected in this context. But it is music of a formidable intensity. One way in which this is achieved is through the time-honoured Baroque device of piling up imitations. A classic use of it would be Handel's, in the trio 'The flocks shall leave the mountains' from *Acis and Galatea* (which, incidentally, Mozart was coming to know at around this time – he arranged it for performance at Baron van Swieten's academies a few months later – though it would be rash to suggest actual influence). The main theme here, Ex. 26*a*, consists of just such a passage. But Mozart adds to it, when presenting a varied continuation after the first eight bars, his inversion device, used with sublime poetic imagination: Ex. 26*b* shows how he takes the bass of Ex. 26*a* as his starting-point for the violin line of Ex. 26*b* but first gives it a different, more sensuously graceful shape and then lets it acquire a new identity as a counter-theme. The little flick of two demisemiquavers that runs through the movement first appears in this counter-theme, at the point where it takes over the main line of the music. This, in a succession of descending woodwind scales – the relationship with the two-note figure that domi-

Ex.26

K550, ii.1

ii.9

nates the first movement is too obvious to need stressing – serves as counter-theme when the strings resume their imitations. The lyrical second-subject theme (coloured on its repetition by varied woodwind doublings) leads into a brief tutti, another of those characterised by its dark tone, this time with all the strings at the bottom of their compass while the woodwind are fairly high in theirs.

But the expressive climax of the Andante falls in the development: first in the sombre music where strings and wind seem to be vying for primacy, with quaver chords six (or five) times repeated (derived from the opening, Ex. 26*a*) struggling against series of demisemiquaver flicks; and second in the wailing chromatic passages (derived from the bass of Ex. 26*a*) with which the woodwind lead the music back to E♭ for the recapitulation. The beginning of this section sustains the poignancy of what has just passed, with the violins floating off, as if despairingly, into F minor, and the folding together of the main theme's continuation and the transitional material. The rest of the recapitulation, however, follows the exposition closely.

The minuet hardly offers the relaxed, dance-like interlude that might traditionally have been expected. Instead, there are aggressively synco-pated rhythms, three-bar phrases and orchestration that is not exactly crude but is certainly rugged. The second section starts with the open-ing phrase in the lower strings and upper woodwind, several times repeated, while a counter-theme is played on the violins and bassoons: one theme is heard doubled in four octaves, the other in three. When the opening phrase returns in the violins, still over three octaves, it is canoni-cally imitated, also over three. But the trio is another matter. This, the only G major section in the symphony, has almost the feeling of chamber music: gentle, luminous, its phrases gracefully shaped, and using a conventional cadence figure which by its context carries almost a tinge of irony. Mozart did not touch this trio when he came to add the clarinets, so its dialogue of flute, oboes and bassoons stands, with the horns, now paired in G, adding their voices towards the end. Even in the trio, Mozart preserves the pessimistic contour of phrase that pre-dominates throughout the symphony – rising, then falling back – and any sense of repose or balm that might have been afforded by the major-key music is felt to be contradicted.

The finale is the most fiery symphonic movement Mozart composed; his only instrumental movements to compare with it, perhaps, are the finale of the D minor piano concerto, K.466, and the two-piano fugue, K.426 (which incidentally he arranged for strings at just the time he was composing these last three symphonies). The two ideas with which it begins – the *piano* rising arpeggio falling back after its top note, and the *forte* quaver figure that responds to it – dominate the movement. The second of them leads off the tutti that follows, and later is carried down into the basses; it also leads off the closing tutti, after the lyrical second subject.

It is however with the development that the real excitement starts. It fires off with an arpeggio, then tonally disorientating the listener for the moment with chromatic notes. Theorists have made too much of this passage, suggesting that Mozart was moving towards a Schoenbergian twelve-note pattern (the twelve notes of the chromatic scale do in fact appear, once, without any being repeated). Far from leaping from one Viennese School to another yet unborn, Mozart was using a conventional series of diminished sevenths, the most common way of creating tonal ambiguity in his time, in descending fourths, as Ex. 27 shows. Then woodwind descending thirds, exactly paralleling the analogous point in the first movement, lead us safely back to D minor, the dominant key.

Ex.27

But this restless music does not stay there, or anywhere, for long. Soon it moves across the minor keys, to reach F minor, where the violas and first violins embark on a contrapuntal argument over the arpeggio figures and other motifs, with the occasional aggressive note from one or other horn when it can manage to fit in with the harmony. The other strings join in, then the woodwind – with the advantage in this chromatic music of being able to play any note – take over from the horns. Their emphatic contribution, while the strings are counterpointing with increasing urgency, clarifies the tonal progress as the music shifts in descending fourths again, through the minor keys: C–G–D–A–E–B–F♯–C♯. There, at the most distant possible point from G minor, the music pauses. Mozart intentionally strains to the limit, if not beyond, the capacity of the listener to retain an awareness of the home key – a capacity on which the proper comprehension of tonal music critically depends. We are, presumably, intended to struggle to avoid losing our bearings altogether. And the next page of the symphony makes it no easier, for the music modulates with such alarming violence and rapidity over eleven bars that it is almost impossible to follow. It then lands, emphatically, in a new key, and the recapitulation begins – and we are glad enough to trust Mozart to have got us to the right place at the right time.

The recapitulation itself is fairly orderly, but not without a number of details that strengthen the impact of the symphony and especially of its unambiguous determination to remain in the minor key (both the piano quartet and the string quintet in G minor end in the major, as too does the D minor piano concerto). The first tutti is reshaped, avoiding the brightening that even a glimpse of a major key can provide; and there are several changes in the second-subject theme – on its first (string) statement more chromaticism in the harmony and a more tortuous line, and in the second (wind) a poignant descending chromatic scale on the accompanying bassoon, a distant 'Neapolitan' harmony and a more chromatic line. The pathos created by the rehearing of a once major-key melody in the minor is pressed the more firmly home. Otherwise, the only significant change is a modest eight-bar expansion of the coda to add to its finality.

It may seem surprising that Mozart indicates repeats for both halves of this movement, especially as much of the effect of the development section depends on its unexpectedness. It seems clear, however, that in these late works – for the E♭ symphony and the last of all, No. 41 in C, like the G minor, have both repeats indicated in their finales but only the expositions in their first movements – Mozart was consciously moving towards giving greater weight to his finales. This may be seen as a gradual tendency in his symphonies over the years, and indeed in other works too; the idea of a cheerful romp to end with was becoming increasingly alien as time, and the world around him, moved on. The path is a clear one, though not of course a smooth one in this respect, from the early symphonies of Haydn and those of Mozart's youth to, ultimately, Beethoven's Choral Symphony, with its vast, momentous last movement. The Romantic finale occupies an altogether different role from that of the era when symphonies were written to gratify the ears of princes.

Mozart's last symphony, No. 41, K.551, is a milestone on this path. As we shall see, its finale earned it the title, in Germany, of 'Symphony with fugue-finale'. It is also, of course, known as the 'Jupiter', a title probably bestowed on it in the early years of the nineteenth century by Johann Peter Salomon, the German-born London impresario and violinist who was responsible for the genesis of Haydn's last twelve symphonies.

The 'Jupiter' is a grandly spacious work, squarely in the tradition of Mozart's C major, trumpets-and-drums symphonies, but far beyond any of them in its expressive scope. Its opening seems to echo, with its contrast of *forte* and *piano* (Ex. 28), the old J. C. Bach type; or perhaps it is as close to some imaginary opera scene in which the inexorable voice of authority (figure *x*) is answered with gentle pleas (*y*). When the opening music is repeated, after a martial tutti (with flourishes akin to *x* within the texture), there are counter-themes in the woodwind. All these ideas, though strongly characterised in themselves, have a motivic nature that promises further development; for *y* this begins in the next tutti, as it is repeated with increasing urgency, the first violins on top, and a middle voice of second violins with bassoons and – exceptionally – the cellos, for once uncoupled from the double-basses so that they can add their intense voices within the orchestral texture. Mozart's tutti writing in his mature symphonies holds endless variety and fascination.

Ex.28

K551, i.1 (tutti in 8ves)   (strings)

The first of the second-subject themes is strikingly original in cast and in its sense: graceful, skittish in its rhythms, yet wholly serious. Part-way through, a bassoon joins the violins, then a flute too, a typically Mozartian subtle variation of timbre. Equally subtle is the phrase structure, $2+4$, $2+4+4$ (and a continuation, $4+4$) – the first four-bar phrase, seemingly complete in itself initially, acquiring a counter-phrase second time that gives it a fuller sense. Then, after another tutti using figure *y*, this time at double speed, comes a new theme, which Mozart borrowed from an aria, 'Un bacio di mano', which he had written three months before for insertion in a comic opera (by Anfossi). Curiously, he again has the bassoon, then bassoon and flute, doubling the violins; and the cellos, once more unshackled from the double-basses, supply the 'Alberti'-type accompaniment. Beyond dispute, this theme is in the *opera buffa* style (the words associated with it in the aria are 'Voi siete un po' tondo, mio caro Pompeo, l'usanze del mondo andate a studiar' – 'You are a bit dense, my dear Pompey; go and study the ways of the world'). Frivolous words: but the theme has a motivic character, and this is the one that Mozart principally uses in the development – first, a simple presentation in the distant key of E♭, then in dialogues and imitations between violins and lower strings, with growing urgency, until the music settles on the dominant of A minor. What at first seems like a recapitulation – except that it is in F, not C – turns out to be the beginning of a further, still more violent phase of the development, based on the opening flourish (*x* of Ex. 28) and its variants; but for all its wildness this passage does lead back to the home key, where after a further reminder of the *opera buffa* theme the recapitulation arrives. This is quite regular, with an interesting diversion into the minor key and towards the flat side of C major when Ex. 28 appears with its counter-theme, and a marked heightening of the tutti in the middle of the second subject, also with an unexpected modulation that momentarily threatens to carry the music too far afield.

The Andante cantabile (the direction is rare in Mozart) shows several of the features we have seen in others of his late slow movements. But it begins with a gentle, sublimely poised theme, on muted violins, like nothing else in Mozart (or of course any other composer) with the pained floridity of its winding line. Again, the scoring is worth noticing: oboes double the violins when they are *forte*, flute and bassoon supply the softer additional colouring when they are *piano*. At once the theme is taken up – though only its first four bars – by the basses, freeing the violins to weave a line in counterpoint with it. Then the music turns to the minor, and the tutti that follows is dark in tone with high first violins and woodwind but low middle strings. But the skies clear – indeed the music even recalls Orpheus's 'Che puro ciel!' ('How clear the skies!'), from Gluck's opera, as he steps from the underworld into the Elysian Fields. What follows is certainly one of Mozart's most heavenly pages: a simple sequential theme on violins and woodwind, then a succession of harmonies of almost unbearable sweetness in support of an eloquent though again unusually florid line – and this is repeated, further elaborated and enriched, with the second violins' harmonic figures taking on new life as a counterpoint to the melody.

The brief development section is little more than a fuller and more impassioned working of the tutti from the exposition. And if the development hardly develops, the recapitulation is fairly reluctant to recapitulate. In its second bar, the basses intervene with the counterpoint to the opening theme heard earlier on the violins. This seems to act almost as a provocation: the violins take it up and prolong it, then the basses do so, and the two groups appear to vie in this flowing music with increasing passion, while the wind instruments punctuate with a rhythmic figure of their own. A great climax is reached – and subsides to lead into the second subject, which is regularly recapitulated. And then, at what ought to have been the end, Mozart, harking back to procedures he used in symphonies of nearly two decades earlier, and revived in a somewhat different way in No. 39 in E♭, gives us again the movement's principal theme (or much of it), which we have not heard in full since the beginning. The woodwind intervene, with a version of the earlier violin counterpoint, but their phrases stop short; and the beautiful, long-breathed continuation now acquires, from its obvious proximity to the end of the movement, a new patina of nostalgia.

The minuet here must surely be the most truly symphonic of all minuets of the eighteenth century. Its first phrase, four notes chromatically descending, supports the entire movement: as its 'second subject' (in bar 9), for most of the eleven bars of its 'development', in the continuing development that comprises most of the 'recapitulation' (where it appears in the basses, then as the substance of an eight-bar imitative passage for the woodwind). *Ars celare artem*: the music seems cheerful, spirited and shapely but is also the product of the most refined and enterprising compositional process. The trio, a graceful interlude with elegant bows or curtseys, serves as a perfect foil.

The 'fugue-finale' is not, of course, simply a fugue, in a Bachian sense, or (more relevantly) in the sense that some of Haydn's Op. 20 string quartet finales, or Mozart's in his K.168 and K.173 quartets of 1773, are. These, along with the two-piano fugue that Mozart had just arranged for strings, are fugal from beginning to end. Mozart and his contemporaries wrote another kind of fugal movement, one that uses fugue within a sonata-form type of movement; the outstanding example is the finale of Mozart's K.387 string quartet (1782), the first of his set dedicated to Haydn. Other composers, notably Michael Haydn, wrote this type, in chamber works and in symphonies; Mozart certainly knew symphonies by Michael Haydn with fugal finales, and once noted down the opening bars of such a movement. So the concept of the 'Jupiter' finale did not spring from his head fully armed: it belonged squarely in an Austrian tradition. Nevertheless, taking Mozart's music in isolation, a fugal finale represents a natural outcome of the tendencies we have already seen in his late symphonic works: his readiness to use contrapuntal writing in a variety of ways to enrich the texture, to tauten the structure, to intensify the expression. All of these he does triumphantly in the more rigorous and methodical application of contrapuntal techniques in this marvellous movement.

It begins innocently enough, with the four-note phrase (Ex. 29*a*) that we touched on during the discussions of K.45b and 319 (pp. 19 and 60–61, and which may possibly have been foreshadowed in the trio of the minuet. This phrase has a long ancestry. It seems to be related to various plainchant melodies and, notably, a hymn *Lucis creator* from a collection much used by Austrian composers working in the tradition of J. J. Fux, the Viennese Kapellmeister early in the century whose teaching had so profound an influence up to Beethoven's generation and indeed beyond (his approach to the study of counterpoint is still widely favoured). Mozart, as we have seen, used the phrase in earlier symphonies; it also appears in sacred works, notably the Mass, K.192, where it is set to the words 'Credo, credo' and (in a manner popular in Austrian mass settings) recurs many times over. Here it first appears as the beginning of an eight-bar theme, which is repeated in part in a tutti – where there are bass flourishes recalling those in the exactly analogous passage in the first movement. The tutti also proclaims an important idea (Ex. 29*b*) based on a descending scale. Then comes the 'fugue', or what in modern terminology we would call a fugal exposition, in five voices (the double-basses, as so often in this symphony, are briefly independent of the cellos), with the first three notes of Ex. 29*a* as the fugue subject. In a further tutti a new phrase (Ex. 29*c*) is introduced, and overlapping presentations of Ex. 29*b* lead to a cadence and the second subject, more lyrical in character (Ex. 29*d*). But the material of the first subject refuses to be banished, Exx. 29*b* and *c* insisting that they belong here too, and there is also a new tag on the oboes (Ex. 29*e*). When Ex. 29*c* threatens to take over, the second-subject theme abandons its lyricism and asserts itself powerfully, in close imitations, first in two voices and then, still closer, in four. Now, as so often at this juncture, Mozart brings back material from the first subject to draw the exposition firmly together – first the continuation of Ex. 29*a*, but then, more emphatically, the scales of Ex. 29*b*, now in inverted imitation (the violins go upwards, the lower strings downwards). It is with these scales, *piano* on a solitary oboe and bassoon, that the exposition ends.

After this excitement, the development begins with gentle meditation around the four-note theme and the scales as the music finds its

Ex.29

(a) Molto Allegro

K551, iv.1

(b)

iv.19 [ƒ]

(c)

iv.56 [ƒ]

(d)

iv.74

(e)

iv.76

way into a new key. Then, suddenly, it takes fire, with more, still denser imitative treatment of the scale theme, sometimes upwards, sometimes downwards, sometimes beginning in one direction and continuing in another. This is on the strings, who draw from the woodwind chromatic complaints based on the four-note theme; the strings break off, in E minor, and a deft chromatic switch, with the bassoons slipping down a semitone from a dominant chord in the one key to a dominant seventh in the other, eases the music back into C major and the recapitulation.

But the reassurance is short-lived. After the violence of what has passed, nothing can be the same; an exact repetition of exposition material would betoken an innocence that is now unreal. So it is not surprising when the full orchestra, though *piano*, adds its voice after a couple of bars. But it is surprising, in fact alarming, when the ensuing tutti veers off into violent chromaticisms – the violins relentlessly pursuing the four-note theme, the basses careering around with their flourishes, the woodwind wailing in unison chromatics. The music seems out of control. But before too long it is back to regularity. This desperate passage is, in fact, a substitution for the fugue exposition we had before, which could scarcely have been repeated now without seeming almost comically tautologous: its earlier function was to introduce the style of the movement in a controlled context, and that is now no longer necessary. The replacement passage, following many precedents in earlier symphonies, serves as extra development and reinforcement of the home key by heightening its desirability after these tonal wanderings. After that, the recapitulation is almost exact, except at its climactic point where what in the exposition has been a passing chromaticism is now sustained much longer – to powerful effect: again, a technique we have noted before, in slightly different forms (for example in the first movement of the Prague Symphony).

But the music does not end here. Mozart rarely wrote substantial codas, as we have seen; often some eight bars or so serve to provide an appropriate air of finality. But a movement like this one needs more, and Mozart had prepared his ground for a truly resplendent peroration. There is a *piano* passage, slightly mysterious, using an inversion of the four-note theme: it is analogous to the music at the beginning of the development. Then (Ex. 30) the violas, *forte*, lead off with Ex. 29*d*, against *a* in the cellos (with bassoons and horns) – and this heralds a passage in which Exx. 29*a*, *b*, *c*, *d* and *e* are presented simultaneously, several times over in a variety of vertical permutations: it is not only a *tour de force* of counterpoint – Mozart had, of course, devised his themes with the idea of combining them in mind – but also, far beyond that, a

Ex.30

iv.387

99

Ex. 30–contd.

truly magnificent effect, overwhelming in its concentrated display of the movement's material in a glitteringly brilliant fabric of sound. After that, music from the first pages of the movement carries it through to the end, with a fanfare of trumpets, horns and timpani bringing the 'Jupiter' to a conclusion of due nobility – and, with it, Mozart's symphonic output. This movement truly sounds like the last word: sad that we can never know in what direction Mozart might have moved onward, happy that we can never conceive the possibility of his excelling it.

Index of Symphonies

*Not authentic.